Spiritual Clarity

Jackie Wellman

PublishAmerica
Baltimore

© 2005 by Jackie Wellman.
All rights reserved. No part of this book may be reproduced, stored in a retrieval system or transmitted in any form or by any means without the prior written permission of the publishers, except by a reviewer who may quote brief passages in a review to be printed in a newspaper, magazine or journal.

First printing

ISBN: 1-4137-7654-X
PUBLISHED BY PUBLISHAMERICA, LLLP
www.publishamerica.com
Baltimore

Printed in the United States of America

Imagine there's no heaven; it's easy if you try
No hell below us, above us only sky
Imagine all the people living for today...

Imagine there's no countries; it isn't hard to do
Nothing to kill or die for, and no religion too
Imagine all the people living life in peace...

— "Imagine" copyright 1971 Lenono Music

Dedication

This book is dedicated to my husband Mark, who did not laugh. Mark, you are my rock—emotionally and physically. I really appreciate your support in my effort to write this book, especially since our views are very different. Mark was my official pre-editing editor, and he has wonderful forearms!

My parents, who taught me the important lesson that being a good person is the main goal in life, this book is part of that lesson and is for you. My mother suggested I write this book; before her suggestion, it had never crossed my mind that I could write anything. My father, who took on the roles of father and grandfather when he did not have to, played the parts beautifully.

I would also like to dedicate this to my son, Matt, who is the main reason I wanted answers. Matt even took part in editing; his suggestion of *prefer* instead of *rather* made a difference. Matt—Peace, love, groovy, dig to you!

Acknowledgments

I would like to thank everyone who talked to me about religion. They helped me to understand various aspects of religion and what it means to them.

A special thank you goes to Bruce Robinson of Religioustolerance.org, who always promptly answered my questions and told me just what I needed to know. I would also like to thank those who read the book before it was published for their ideas. I especially want to thank Margaret Todd, the first person to read this book besides me. She made a scary experience not so bad and gave me several ideas to improve what I had.

My mom was so enthusiastic; I truly appreciate her support. She was more excited than I was. She is my biggest fan.

PublishAmerica—thank you for the chance.

Table of Contents

Section I—Why a Search?	13
Section II—Religion Rundown	25
What Is Religion?	29
Religion's Purpose	30
Christianity	33
Catholicism	37
Episcopalian	38
Lutheran	38
Presbyterian	39
Methodist	39
Baptist	39
Congregationalist	39
United Reformed Church	40
Evangelicals	40
Pentecostal	40
Mennonites	41
Unitarian Universalists	41
Latter-Day Saints	41
Holiness Movement	42
Christian Science	42
Jehovah's Witness	43
Seventh-Day Adventists	43
Quakers	44
Salvation Army	44
Amish	44
Church of Christ	45
Shakers	45
World Church of the Creator	46

New Age	46
Baha'i	46
Freemason	47
Unification Church	47
Wicca	48
International Society for Krishna Consciousness	48
Transcendental Meditation	48
Sikhism	49
Islam	50
Jainism	53
Zoroastrians	54
Rastafarianism	54
Caodaism	54
Judaism	55
Confucianism	59
Taoism	59
Shinto	60
Roma	61
Vodun	62
Buddhism	62
African Religions	64
Hinduism	64
Santeria	66
Native American Spirituality	67
Satanism	67
Kabbalah	68
Bibliography	69
Section III—Evolution and Common Sense	71
The Facts	75
Radioactive Aging	76
Pangaea	77
Life	78
Our Direct Ancestors	79
Homo sapiens	80
Genetics	81

Gradualism	82
Evolution in Action	83
Darwin	83
The Truth	85
Bibliography	91
Section IV—In the Name of Religion	93
Religious Intolerance	97
The Crusades	102
The Inquisition	104
Jewish Persecution	107
Witch-hunts	111
Natives	113
Colonists	118
Slave Trade	121
Recent Intolerance	122
Bibliography	126
Section V—Clarity	129
Heaven and Hell	133
Where Was God?	134
Women	138
It Says That?	140
Violence in the Bible	143
The Tale of an Ark	144
Stem Cells	146
My Clarity	149
Bibliography	157

Why a Search?

Let no one be proud of their birth.
Know that we are all born of the same clay.
-Guru Nanak-Sikh

If anyone says "I love God" and hates his brother, he is a liar: for he who does not love his brother whom he has seen, cannot love God for whom he has not seen.
-John's First Letter

What do we live for if not to make life easier or less difficult for each other?
-George Elliot

The truth shall make you free.
-John's Gospel

The world is so exquisite, with so much love and moral depth, that there is no reason to deceive ourselves with pretty stories for which there's little good evidence. Far better, it seems to me, in our vulnerability, is to look at death in the eye and to be grateful every day for the brief magnificent opportunity that life provides.
-Carl Sagan, *Cosmos*

The Queen of the Klutzes. A real clod! Not graceful in the slightest. Those have always been ways to describe me. I was never any good at sports, the last kid to get picked for teams in gym class. Aren't you supposed to quit getting skinned knees as frequently when you reach adulthood? Or at least not get as many bruises and scabs as the average child does? People even used me as something to joke about because I could always be counted on to trip. I even laughed about it. It never crossed my mind that an actual medical problem could exist, even though my grandmother, two of her brothers, a second cousin, my uncle, and an aunt had an incurable genetic degenerative spinal cord disorder. It never occurred to me because for a dominant genetic problem, your parents must have it and my mom was free and clear. Did I have an ultimate case of denial or what? Talk about a rose tinted world.

I actually thought that my extreme morning stiffness had to do with aging. But your average 32-year-old is not so muscle stiff that they walk like Frankenstein. I was really grasping at straws. Things gradually got worse. I really did not feel as though things in my body were working like they should. Certain things were beginning to get more difficult. Since I had no idea what was going on, most of these things I kept to myself for a long time. I remember going for a walk on the bike trail with my mom; my feet were making lots of noise, shuffling and clodding along. My mom said, "Pick up your feet," and I realized that I could not do it. I could not walk without being incredibly noisy. Just going for a short walk made me miserably tired, just plain exhausted. I thought I was just horribly out of shape. At this time I was not routinely exercising. I thought the reason my legs were not working right was lack of exercise. So I started to work out. The exercise did help, but my balance still was not right. I tried lots of things, stepped out of my comfort zone. Before this I was guilty, as many of us are, of taking the path of least resistance. Now I am an exercise junky; even though it is hard, I feel better making myself do it.

One day a nurse from Dr. Fink's office at the University of Michigan called. Dr. Fink is trying to find a cure for hereditary spastic paraplegia; he is the guru of research for the hereditary spastic paraplegia/primary lateral sclerosis community. Hereditary spastic paraplegia is the disease that kept my grandmother in a wheelchair at the end of her life, my uncle in a wheelchair most of the time and my aunt in leg braces. The doctor was lining up people from families of hereditary spastic paraplegia sufferers to donate blood for research. Of course, I was definitely not affected by hereditary spastic paraplegia myself but would be willing to do whatever I could to help the affected family members, anything to bring Dr. Fink closer to finding a cure.

The nurse started asking questions about my family's medical history and my own medical history. She moved on. "Have you personally experienced any symptoms?" Hereditary spastic paraplegia is rare; its symptoms and age of onset vary from person to person. My grandmother did not really experience any severe symptoms until she was older, so I never suspected it. My aunt and uncle are older than me. My mom was not a sufferer. I thought I was good to go. I was unaware of any other symptoms besides trouble walking. I was unaware of anyone my age having symptoms. Basically, I was just plain unaware. In the view through my tunnel vision denial glasses, I could see no connection between excessive clumsiness and a neurological disorder. My answer to the question concerning symptoms let the nurse in on the fact that I was not fully aware of what all could be involved. Ignorance was definitely not bliss. When she went on to describe symptoms, I could feel my heart beating faster and my eyes started to water. As she went through the list of symptoms, it was a shock to me that a lot of my answers were "yes." My emotions were going berserk. Did this mean I was going to be confined to a wheelchair like my grandma? At one point, when asked if the soles of my shoes wore out toe first, I actually got to my son's shoes as fast as I could. I felt an enormous sense of relief when those wonderful heels were worn down and the front part looked good. My shoes never last long, the front part wears out, but I thought dragging my toes was just a bad habit of mine. Toe drop, causing tripping, is one of the first detectable signs. Joan Mathay, Dr. Fink's nurse, told me that my son would have a fifty percent chance of getting hereditary spastic paraplegia if I had it.

I came to the conclusion that maybe I should look into this HSP thing a bit further. The first two doctors I spoke to were family practice physicians. The first said, "That is caused from syphilis." I was quick to respond, "My grandma does not have syphilis!" The second said, "I have heard of it but that is the extent of my knowledge." This second doctor referred me to a neurologist who had seen one other hereditary spastic paraplegia patient. Now I know that there are only an estimated 20,000 hereditary spastic paraplegia or primary lateral sclerosis patients in the United States. There is a non-profit volunteer-run foundation representing these two diseases because they are very similar.

Before seeing me, Dr. Rankin ordered an MRI to rule out multiple sclerosis, which has similar symptoms. I began to worry when it was MRI time. My husband refers to this as "obsessing." I do admit to excessive worrying but when your brain is scanned, who knows what could be found? Maybe a tumor was causing all of the clumsiness. I have a lot of headaches, so a tumor made sense to me. It is a strange feeling knowing that you are being checked for brain malfunctions.

When it was time for my appointment, I was still in a strong denial mode, feeling sure that she would just give me a mimeographed sheet of paper outlining a few exercises to make things all better. I took the MRI results and the pictures to the neurologist, feeling a little uneasy; after all, these were photos of my brain. But it looked good to me…there probably is a reason I am not a neurologist. There was a barrage of neurological tests: the thumb to each finger over and over again, pushing down with my toes, pushing up with my toes, running up and down the hall, walking heel-to-toe, etc. The strangest was when using a vibrating tool, like a tuning fork that was used in music class, the doctor placed it on my hand so I could feel the vibrations. After telling me to tell her when it was done vibrating, she placed it on my big toe. When the sensation stopped I told her; she then moved the tool to where I could see it; it was still moving! At that moment I felt like someone had punched me in the face. Bummer! With my MRI results, my positive family history and my failure at the neurological testing—which I know I could have done better on if I was given adequate time to study, she confirmed what I had been denying all along, that I had a degenerative spinal cord disorder—hereditary spastic paraplegia. I have to admit, I felt a little stupid for not even suspecting it. Maybe I did, I just did want to admit it to myself or anyone else.

My worst fear was that it would not end with me, that I would pass it on to my son. The only information about HSP that I could find was on the Internet. My search led me to an Internet listserv, a way people can communicate with each other about HSP and PLS. There are members throughout the world. Dr. Fink is also on the list. He adds valuable input whenever needed and announces any new discoveries in his lab that are helping to bring a cure closer. On the listserv, when you write an e-mail it goes out to everyone on the list. On the list things are discussed from the best canes to stem cell research and many things in between. A foundation was formed with people from the list, and fundraising is done to support research. The foundation is The Spastic Paraplegia Foundation; it can be found on the Internet at http://www.sp-foundation.org/. Rare diseases are much harder to get research money for because not many even know about HSP or PLS. We have no Michael J. Fox or Montel Williams to speak for us.

Now, a little about hereditary spastic paraplegia; it is actually a spinal cord disorder. The ends of the nerves that send impulses from the brain and back to the brain are degenerating. These impulses travel from nerve to nerve across axons and dendrites until they reach the desired muscle and tell it to move, where to move to, how to move, how fast to move, etc. So nothing is actually wrong with my legs; the message to move or keep warm is just having trouble making it all the way down to my toes. As the area of degeneration gets larger, the area not receiving messages from the brain will increase. Anything involving the feet requires extra effort to achieve the correct and coordinated movement. I explain it to those who ask by using the example of walking across a room. For most people, you just tell yourself to walk across the room and it basically takes no effort. For someone with HSP, every step has to be thought about and extra energy exerted to make it work. Fatigue is an ever-present symptom. Another symptom is loss of balance. To keep your balance, muscles are continuously being used, working together to maintain an upright position. We are not even aware of these signals and the muscle contraction/relaxation that continually goes on. Since these messages from the brain are not getting to where they should in time, balance is compromised. At this time my problems are mainly just lower legs and feet, affecting balance, and I get the added bonus of a slight slurring of my speech. I am not sure why that symptom is thrown in but it is. It gets much worse when I am tired or cold, as all my symptoms do. There is also muscle cramping and fairly constant cold feet. I do not fully understand the circulation part, but I know that it is present. There is no medication and no method of treatment at this point. The only thing that really seems to help the stiffness and cramping is stretching and exercise.

One day on the listserv someone sent a posting to the listserv declaring that it must be part of God's plan that we all got HSP, so it was okay. God wills it. Bull! The genes got goofed up somewhere along the line; that is why HSP is present. A mutation developed and is unfortunately passed on to fifty percent of the offspring of anyone affected. When I hear someone say, "It must be God's plan; we just do not understand," it gets my blood boiling. How could God be involved in possibly giving my beautiful son HSP? What possible benefit could there be for Matthew to have HSP? Is God into cruelty? I do not think so. God has more important things to do than worry about who gets sick and who does not. Accidents happen. If a person gets hit by a car while crossing the street, it is just horrible timing, not some part of some cruel plan. Thinking that God controls everything would mean God is a homicidal maniac who controls a gigantic Hot Wheels track in the sky. I do not think so. He has more important things to do.

I have always believed in a higher power, that higher power being God. I cannot believe that God controls everything. He is not cruel. He does not want me to have HSP.

My mother was a churchgoer as a child. She had a few negative experiences that started several resentments towards organized religions. For example, when her father died, she was eight years old. She was told that God wanted him and he was in a better place. The typical eight-year-old would question this and wonder what was wrong with the place he was in. How can God be so vicious as to take away an eight-year-old's father? An eight-year-old would have enough to process without hearing these comments. Although, I am sure that that is a standard response to death and the comments were meant in kindness, to help a child through a dreadful time. It is challenging to explain tragedy by invoking God's will.

My biological father is Jewish. Born in Israel, his family moved to America when he was seven. He was off to the West Coast soon after my parents were divorced, when I was six. Weekend visitations and synagogues were not a part of my past. My mother remarried and I was raised by a man who did not go to church every Sunday, but did live by the Golden Rule. He stepped in when my real father stepped out and has been there ever since. He is still around daily and is a wonderful grandfather for my son.

Questions have always been on my mind and never answered to my satisfaction. The desire was always present, the longing to be able to accept and believe. In fact, it was very strong. I always felt I was missing some integral part since I did not feel like others did about faith. I could not understand why I had such a hard time with the whole religion thing. I never understood how something could be believed fully when proof to the contrary was right in front of the eyes. Blind faith over intellectual reasoning seems non-negotiable.

The questions constantly plagued me; some were even silly: If there is a heaven, wouldn't it be overcrowded by now? What about all of those babies and people of other religions, different than Christianity, do they all go to hell? Does anyone who is sane actually believe purgatory is real? Why, if religion is so good, do so many people die in the name of religion? Why can't women be priests? Why can't priests marry? It seems obvious that something is wrong with the Catholic priest system since there are so many child molesters within the Church. What is wrong with birth control? Isn't birth control better than unwanted babies? The Catholic Church or any other form of religion opposing birth control seems to say…we are opposed to using common sense. Why is there so much resentment toward the Jews? Jesus was Jewish. How can "the plan" include my son getting HSP? What kind of a plan is that? Nothing I want any part of. Could religion just be a comforting way to deal with some type of loss or suffering? Can't you just say a prayer wherever you are; why does it need to be on a Sunday morning in a church? Does God listen better on Sundays? Why do some people just assume that only the best people go to church every week? I found a perfect response to that one in a book by Fritz Ridnour titled *So What's the Difference*. It said, "Going to church on a regular basis no more makes you a Christian than going to McDonald's makes you a hamburger."

On a search for some answers was where I decided to go. I tried church many times, even taught a little Sunday school. Church seemed to serve a purpose for many, a bond with others who think the same. I never actually felt good about going; I was more concerned with the yard work that I could be getting done during the service. My husband's family church is Episcopalian, so communion was every Sunday. Whenever I take communion, my main concern is getting it over without anyone noticing my limp. This is not the way church is supposed to affect you. What was wrong with me, that church was not fulfilling for me like it was for others? I never got past the point of going just because it was something I *should* do instead of enjoying it. I never understood why on Sunday mornings people should be in church as opposed to anywhere else. Why that makes them better people. It seemed that a lot of people who attend church regularly were not such Good Samaritans the other six days of the week. Does one day, out of seven, make up for the other six? Do some people really think that it is justifiable to sin if you go to church and ask for forgiveness? I always thought it was the other way around; we all sin, some more others. You pray for forgiveness and try to correct the behavior. Not attend church once a week so you sin all you want.

All of these questions seemed to be in my daily thoughts. Now I needed to find some answers.

It was always a mystery to me how anyone could be satisfied with his or her present amount of knowledge about anything. I read books and articles from each of the many viewpoints about religion to get a more complete understanding of how religion affects people, studied the different kinds of religions, and asked a lot of questions. Basically, all of this was how I achieved spiritual clarity. I really do think that after 37 years I finally get it.

Religion Rundown

De gustibus non est disputum.
-Latin, for personal taste is not debatable.

I have a dream that my four children will one day live in a nation where they will not be judged by the color of their skin but by the content of their character.
-Martin Luther King, Jr.

The responsibility of tolerance lies with those who have a wider vision.
-George Elliot

There will be peace on earth when there is peace among the world religions.
-Hans Kung

Difference of opinion in religion is helpful.
-Thomas Jefferson

All races and tribes in the world are like different flowers of one meadow. All are beautiful. As children of the creator they must all be respected.
-taken from the Native American Traditional Code of Ethics

I used to think anyone doing anything weird was weird. Now I know that it is the people that call others weird that are weird.
-Paul McCartney

It is the duty of every cultured man or woman to read sympathetically the scriptures of the world. If we are to respect others' religions as we would have them respect our own, a friendly study of the world's religions is a sacred duty.
-Mahatma Gandhi

What Is Religion?

Religion is defined in many ways; no one definition fully includes all religions except perhaps this one—religion is one's beliefs. But that really does not tell you much, so I will list several other definitions.

- Religion is a guide for self-improvement
- Religion is belief in a higher power
- Religion promotes directions for achieving happiness
- Religion teaches morality
- Religion explains man to man
- Religion helps explain tragedies
- Religion defines relationships between people and the rest of the universe
- Religion defines relationships between people and the creator of the universe

These are just a few definitions. Religion probably has a different meaning for everyone. Religion is the belief in something beyond the physical world. It usually, but not always, involves worshipping a higher unseen power, which is thought to have created the world and now oversees it. Religion is more than just a belief in a god or gods, for many it is a way of life, a tradition. It is a method used to find a peaceful life amidst a world of chaos.

Religion offers a community of fellow believers who think about some things in a similar manner. To be surrounded by people who think as you do is comforting. Most people seek out groups or individuals who think like they do. It is often a needed, reassuring tradition for many people to go to a place of worship once a week or more. In any religious gathering you are surrounded by people with the same religious heritage as you. It is comforting to be with and talk to like-minded individuals.

All forms of religion offer some type of moral education or rules for behavior, a basic moral code, like the Golden Rule. The opportunity to make a wrong choice is always there but the presence of religion will hopefully make the decision to do the right thing a little easier. Lots of people have difficulty defining what to do or what not to do; religion can help with this. Some people need more guidance than others. It is mystifying that anyone would need to be told how to determine the difference between right and wrong but apparently some do. Religion can help with this. A few religions have lots of rules and that is perfect for followers who need that. Most religions send out a message of love and compassion. The ways those messages are sent out are a little different, but they basically all say the same thing—be nice!

Religion's Purpose

In the research I did for this book, I read many things that people believed religion did for them. Among those was a man who said he had not given up on his marriage yet because of religion. A woman talked about how she now thought about money differently; she now looked for ways to help the poor instead of just buying things for herself. A few people just naturally want to help others any way they can but apparently others need a little guidance, and religion offers that. Another woman talked about faith, saying that some people have said that faith was just a crutch. Then she made the profound statement that for a crippled person there is only one thing worse than a crutch and that is no crutch. This statement especially hits home when dealing with the possibility of an actual crutch or cane in the near future.

Religion answers the big questions for us. For example, what is the purpose for living? How did we get here? Where are we going? Why are we here? How did the Earth get here? According to many religions, if people believe and follow teachings, they will be saved.

Religion also makes death not so final and scary. If you were facing death or a loved one was, the path would be a little smoother truly believing that you or that loved one were headed for bigger and better things instead of the alternative, which would be just being buried six feet under. Religion reduces fear and is a way to help cope with our difficult world. Genuine faith in God can reduce anxiety about life's important events.

There are many words in the English language that pertain just to religion; here are just a few:

- A **pagan** is a person who is not Christian, Jew or Muslim.
- A **heretic** is a believer who maintains religious views contrary to his or her church.
- **Heresy** is any belief or theory that is strongly at variance with established beliefs.
- **Doctrine** is any particular opinion taught by a religion.
- **Orthodox** is conforming to traditional or established doctrine.
- **Gentile** a non-Jewish person, especially a Christian.
- A **heathen** is an unconverted person who does not recognize the God of Christians, Jews or Muslims.
- **Gospel** is the teachings of Jesus and his followers.
- **Ecumenical** promotes greater understanding and tolerance among the various branches of the Christian religions.
- **Monotheistic** is a religion having one God, like Christianity, Judaism or Islam.
- **Pantheistic** is a religion that believes that everything has a spirit. God is not a single entity but the essence of the entire universe.
- **Polytheistic** is a religion that believes in the existence of many gods and goddesses.
- **Trinity** is a belief that a single God has three aspects. As Christianity believes the Trinity is formed by the Father, Son and Holy Spirit.
- **Agnostics** have reached no conclusion as to whether or not God exists.
- **Atheists** totally reject the possibility that God exists.

If we learn about different religions and realize the potential of various religions to produce good people, we can respect the diversity. One thing I learned, and was shocked about, was the many ways different religions resemble each other. Ignorance leads believers to think that their own religion is the only correct way to think and all other beliefs are incorrect. This way of thinking is one of the ways that religion can be dangerous or evil by claims of absolute truth and blind obedience. In history, as long as there has been contact between different religious traditions, there has been misunderstanding and conflict. Once we know about religions other than our own, we can develop an appreciation and respect for other beliefs.

I was very surprised at how little some people I talked to actually knew about ceremonies and traditions in their own church. This I perceived as clearly a situation where people are not thinking for themselves, just playing follow the leader. Asking certain questions brought the "I don't know" answers. "I don't know" is not an acceptable answer for me. How can someone go to church and participate in ceremonies and not know why what is being done is being done? Seems a bit hypocritical.

The following section contains an extremely brief and fundamental description of several religions. The descriptions are presented in an easy to understand manner; so many of the books out there on comparative religion just seem to make everything more confusing. You need to be a religious scholar, whom I am clearly not, to understand them. My fundamental descriptions do not even come close to describing everything out there or everything about the described religions, but the biggies and some of the not so big are briefly mentioned. These descriptions are brief because not many would take the time to learn about some of the things mentioned. Brief is easier to digest. I never took the time until doing this research, which I decided to do to help myself understand religion. I am from a mainly Christian society. I really did not understand the way members of some religions treated members of other religions and why. And I still do not. There are as many religions as types of people. Some groups of people take certain portions of several religions and combine them to create their own religion.

Spirituality can be achieved in almost any religion; you don't even need organized religion. No one can tell you what path is right for you, especially not the government. The descriptions of religion are in no particular order.

Let's learn a little and try to become more tolerant, with not as much self-righteousness. Self-righteousness is a nauseating characteristic.

Christianity

The following information on Christianity is from the Bible, since the Bible tells the Christian story. Christianity was founded by Jesus Christ, also called Jesus of Nazareth or Jesus of Galilee. The only accounts of his life are told in the first four gospels, books in the New Testament, Mark, Matthew, Luke and John.

Jesus was born in Bethlehem, about six miles from Jerusalem. Anybody who celebrates Christmas should know this story. Gabriel, an angel of the Lord, told Mary…a virgin…that she would be having a child, a son to be named Jesus. The child's father was God. Before the baby was born, Mary and her husband, Joseph from Nazareth, were both to travel to Bethlehem. They had to go Bethlehem to pay taxes to the Roman governor. There was no room in the inn, so they spent the night in the stable. Mary gave birth to Jesus.

As an adult, Jesus chose twelve apostles to help him spread the message. Jesus saw himself as having a mission with Judaism. Not only was he a Jew but so was his family and his early followers were Jewish. He spoke as a Jew to Jews. Paul, one of the twelve disciples, compared Christianity to a wild olive branch on the tree of Judaism. *Do all the people who tell Jewish jokes know the man they worship was a Jew who started out preaching Judaism?* It is important to know that Christianity began as a form of Judaism. Jesus followed and preached Jewish scripture…the Old Testament. He originally did not intend to start a new religion. But who knows, maybe that was the plan. As his ministry unfolded, many miracles were attributed to Jesus. He had incredible healing powers.

His ministry was intensely opposed by the Pharisees (a Jewish society of scholars and priests), because of his criticism of hypocrisy within the Jewish community. The Pharisees looked upon Jesus as a rebellion, a young troublemaker. He was accused of breaking the Sabbath because he healed the sick on the day of rest, and he was also accused of blasphemy since he claimed to be the Son of God. Roman authorities...not Jews...got more and more worried about his growing influence over the people, so they planned to get rid of him. Jesus took his disciples to Jerusalem for Passover. On Passover Eve Jesus ate his last supper with his disciples. He was betrayed by Judas Iscariot, one of the twelve disciples. He was arrested by Roman soldiers and brought to Pontius Pilate, the Roman governor. Under Roman law Jesus was convicted of being a political rebel. With a crown of thorns and carrying a cross, Jesus was beaten and led to Golgotha, the place of execution. Jesus was nailed to the cross and left to die.

After he died the body was placed in a tomb. Several days later, some woman came to the tomb to care for the body; they found the tomb empty. The resurrection of Jesus became the foundation of the Christian religion. Jesus was placed on this earth by God to die for our sins. After leaving this earth, if you were a Christian who followed Jesus teaching, eternal life could be achieved.

Christianity is a monotheistic religion. Christians have one God, although his son, Jesus, and the Holy Spirit are part of the trinity. Jesus is not a separate entity but God in human form. God revealed himself in Jesus; through Jesus, Christians get to know God. The Christian religion teaches that Jesus was both man and God, born on Earth to save the human race from its tendency to do wrong. God gave his son to die for our sins and this will redeem people of the Christian faith. Christians teach that everyone is born into sin and can never meet God's standards. Some Christians believe that God singlehandedly created the universe and now controls everything that goes on in it. In Genesis, the beginning of the Bible, God created the heavens and the Earth. On the first day he created light and dark. On the second day the sky was created. The third day, land, seas, and vegetation were added. The fourth day, the stars were created. On the fifth day God added fish to the seas and birds in the skies. The sixth day, animals were added. On the seventh day God rested. That is why Sunday, in the Christian world, is the day of rest. God creates Adam, the first man. From Adam's rib, God created Eve. The whole world is populated from these two. Now the sinning begins. Christians worship the creator, not creation.

In 312 A.D. something dramatic happened. Before that Christians were persecuted. A future Roman emperor named Constantine converted to the Christian faith after he had a vision which told him he would gain a military victory. After defeating his enemy, Constantine assumed political power and issued decrees forbidding the persecution of Christians. His actions made Christianity respectable in the Empire and encouraged conversions to the faith. In 450 A.D., Christianity began to expand and develop.

The Bible is fundamental to the Christian faith; some feel it is a historical document. It contains stories about Jesus from people who knew him and of him. It also contains many of the moral lessons Christians are *supposed* to follow: the Ten Commandments and the Golden Rule. Christians by and large accept the Bible as the divinely inspired word of God.

The Bible contains two main parts, the Old Testament and the New Testament. The Old Testament is also referred to as the Hebrew Bible. The first five books of the Old Testament tell about the beginning of the Jewish (Israelite) culture and race. The next twelve books continue the history of the Israelites. The Israelites moved into the land of Caanan (Palestine) and established a kingdom that lasted almost five hundred years. The next part of the Old Testament is written in poetry form; it includes the Psalms and Proverbs. The last sections are the books of prophets. A prophet is someone who speaks for God.

The New Testament starts out with the gospels. The first four books talk about the life of Jesus; these are Matthew, Mark, Luke and John. The acts talks about the disciples after Jesus was crucified and the resurrection. Then there comes letters from the apostles. The New Testament ends with the revelations, a strange book of visions, symbols and prophecy.

In the fifth and sixth centuries the Roman Empire split in two. In 1054 A.D. there was a dispute between the head of the church in Constantinople and the head of the church in Rome. This lead to what is known as the Schism—a split between the Eastern Orthodox and the Western Roman Catholic religions. In the sixteenth century a reform was started by Martin Luther. The reform was called the Protestant Reform. Martin Luther and another reformist, John Calvin, were opposed to the church because they resented the wealth and power of the Catholic Church. It was a practice of the Church to take money from the people of the congregation in return for the promise of not being punished for sins after death. The reform brought about a fragmentation of Christianity. The reformation replaced the authority of the Roman Catholic Church. Protestantism is a term that covers many religions that came into existence after the reform. Any form of Christianity not adherent of the Roman Catholic faith or of the Eastern Orthodox Church was called Protestant.

Martin Luther also translated the Bible into German. Before that it could only be read in Latin. This loosened the reins on another method of control the church had, because when the Bible was only available in Latin, only a select few could read it. The average commoner did not know Latin; it was a language of the religious elite. It was soon translated into other languages. The invention of the movable type printing press in 1445 by Johannes Gutenburg also made the Bible more accessible to the common man. People could read it for themselves instead of just hearing the church's interpretation. Soon copies were scattered throughout Europe.

Christianity is a diverse faith encompassing many different points of views. I tried to touch on a few of these different kinds of Christian religions.

Christian Holidays

• Lent—a season of repentance and fasting. It begins with Ash Wednesday, the seventh Wednesday before Easter.
• Palm Sunday—the Sunday before Easter when Jesus entered Jerusalem for Passover; crowds called him the savior and scattered palms in his path. Many Christians carry palm fronds on that day.
• Good Friday—the Friday before Easter, the day that Jesus died. A day to remember the fourteen Stations of the Cross, depicting the suffering of Jesus.
• Easter —the most important day of the year for Christians, celebrating the resurrection of Jesus. *I do not know how the Easter Bunny ties in with this one.*
• Pentecost—the seventh Sunday after Easter, commemorating the descent of the Holy Spirit upon the apostles.
• Advent—about a month before Christmas, the time period used to prepare for the arrival of Christ.
• Christmas—December 25 is the day Christians celebrate the birthday of Jesus Christ.
• Epiphany—Wisemen visit the newborn Jesus Christ on January 6.

Catholicism

Roman Catholics accept Jesus Christ as the Son of God. They believe in the trinity; the Father, the Son and the Holy Ghost. They accept and join in specific sacraments. The seven sacraments for Catholics are baptism, confirmation (acceptance into the church, the right to receive communion), Eucharist (communion, sharing in the symbolic sharing of the blood and body of Jesus Christ during mass), penance (confession), the anointing of the sick, marriage and the ordained (clergy). The mother of Jesus is given special honor. *As all mothers should.* Saints are also given special honor. Saints are mortals who have lived out special lives and are always fondly remembered. For example, St. Francis of Assisi is remembered for his special love for animals.

The church is accepted as the place of divine and complete revelation. Acknowledgment of the Pope and bishops of the church as coming directly from Christ is also a Catholic belief. The Pope is given supreme spiritual authority in the Catholic Church.

Catholics believe in the soul being immortal. They feel that each person is responsible for his or her actions. The Roman Catholic faith believes in purgatory.

Catholics even have a special order called the Society of Jesus, whose members are called Jesuits. The aggressive missionary work of the Jesuits is a shining example of modern Catholic history.

Catholics believe that priests and nuns should remain celibate. Symbolically, they are married to God. Although marriage is one of the seven sacraments, priests and nuns are not allowed to marry, at least to a mere mortal.

Episcopalian

The American branch of the Anglican Church or the Church of England. My description of the Episcopal Church is "as close to being Catholic without officially being Catholic." The Episcopal Church does not agree with the authority of the Pope but does agree with the Catholic Church on many issues.

The Episcopal Church and the Catholic Church both use *The Book of Common Prayer*. In 1994 women were finally allowed to become priests in the Episcopal Church. The priests in the Episcopal Church can marry and lead normal lives. The Episcopal Church just recently got a homosexual bishop. Things are really changing, although this could cause a major rift in the Episcopal Church.

Lutheran

Martin Luther was one of the rebels responsible for the Protestant Reformation and the Lutheran Church was the result. Martin Luther criticized the corruption of the Roman Catholic Church and was excommunicated by the Pope, so he started a new religion. The

Lutheran Church was based upon Martin Luther's beliefs. He believed that the teachings of the Bible and an individual's own faith were more important than the church or specific rituals.

Presbyterian

John Calvin founded the Presbyterian Church. He shared many of Martin Luther's beliefs. In addition, he believed in predestination: the idea that God has plans for everyone, including whether being saved is in the picture. This church is based on charity and faith.

Methodist

Methodists got their name from being so methodical. Their goal is to lead ordered, disciplined lives. The Methodist Church is based on individual faith and a responsibility for the improvement of society. Methodists have worldwide ministries and believe in equality of the sexes.

Baptist

Baptist churches do not baptize babies or children. They feel baptism should take place when the adult choice can be made to accept Jesus Christ as your own personal savior. Baptism is an important part of being a Baptist. Baptism in this church involves full immersion in water. The Baptist Church places a lot of importance on the teachings of the Bible and a personal faith.

Congregationalist

Jesus Christ is the head of this church. This religion emphasizes fellowship and cooperation. All churches are independent. Congregationalists honor the Christian community.

United Reformed Church

Congregationalist and Presbyterians, who merged in 1972, make up this church. I included this to show that, basically, if you can get some followers, anyone can open a church.

Evangelicals

The born-again Christians. Protestants who have had an intense conversion experience. Evangelicals are enthusiastic in their efforts to convert others. They stress the importance of the Bible and personal faith in Jesus Christ rather than Christian rituals. The Bible is believed literally. The Book of Revelation (the last part of the Bible) is important in this Christian sect. Evangelicals actually believe that anyone who does not believe as they do will be condemned to hell on Earth and "true Christians" will be taken by God to Heaven at a time called the Rapture. *This sounds like an absolute truth faith. Absolute truth faiths are faiths that believe that they are the only right people and everyone else is highly mistaken. Absolute truth faiths are dangerous; this is how fundamentalists can be created. Scary!*

Pentecostal

Assemblies of God and Church of God in Christ are two Pentecostal churches. These people have also been known as Charismatics. Pentecost services are emotional and spontaneous. There is what is known as speaking in tongues. The workings of the Holy Spirit are important. Great emphasis is placed on man's personal experience with God.

Mennonites

The beginnings of the Mennonite traditions were traced to one of the reform movements called Anabaptism. Menno Simons was the Dutch founder. They felt that church membership must be an adult decision rather than only being baptized as an infant. Mennonites feel that they cannot swear allegiance to an earthly leader and under these grounds cannot serve in the military. They were persecuted for this belief. They cannot, on religious grounds, hold public office. They are known for simple dress and simple living.

Unitarian Universalist Association

They do not believe the Bible is the word of God. They feel that Jesus Christ was a great teacher, not a divine incarnation. There is no trinity. They believe in the oneness of God. Unitarians stay away from rules. Basically, they will take you no matter what you think, Christians and non-Christians. This is the most tolerant and open of the Protestant religions. Unitarians believe in the worth of everyone, acceptance and peace. They feel all religious teachings are inspiring. They feel church rules are restrictive and arrogant. They emphasize understanding rather than a specific faith. Unitarians believe in reason, science and campaigning for human rights. All that is needed is to live a good life and follow the Golden Rule. There is no concern with heaven or hell, just daily living. Man should not look to God for help, but should be his own savior. *This sounds good. This makes a lot of sense.*

Church of Jesus Christ of Latter-Day Saints

The Mormons. I'm sure everyone has had the Mormons knocking on their door at one time or another. They really believe they have a duty to convert others, since only the Mormons will be saved on Judgment Day. They honestly believe that by knocking on your door and bothering you they are saving you. They do have good intentions. Mormons feel they belong to the only true religion. Everyone else is sadly mistaken. *Absolute truth thinking again.* The religion was founded by Joseph Smith, who, when an angel came and dictated it, wrote *The Book of Mormon.* Mormons do believe that the Bible is the word of God. They also believe that they are the "chosen people." Mormons were well-known for the practice of polygamy; only a few communities still do this. Those communities that do still practice polygamy believe that was what God wanted, for a man to have several wives. Polygamy could be beneficial since the object was to populate the world with more Mormons. Because of the practice of polygamy, the Mormons were strongly persecuted. Brigham Young led them west; many settled in Utah. Mormons do not drink alcohol, smoke, drink coffee or tea, and they believe in a strong family unit.

Holiness Movement

The Church of Nazarene is one of the churches in the Holiness Movement. They are dedicated to striving for human perfection. They reject materialistic values and stress the importance of spiritual life. This movement was started by John Wesley, an Anglican priest ordained in 1728. There is a message of sanctification. Some churches ban dancing, alcohol, smoking, foolish talking, playing cards, or marrying unbelievers. In the Holiness Movement, in some of the individual churches, the members are to dress conservatively.

Christian Science

Mary Baker Eddy founded Christian Science in 1875. In this religion she is highly regarded as speaking God's words; she is almost equal to Jesus Christ. She wrote *Science and Health with the Key to the Scriptures,* which is read at services right along with the Bible. The spiritual world is the true reality and the material world is only an illusion. Christian Scientists avoid medicines and medical treatment, because a proper spiritual life will overcome disease and cure illness. *What?? Do they really think a neurological disorder can be prayed away?* Now, as a member, it is acceptable to use a dentist, an optometrist, a doctor for setting broken brokens and a doctor or midwife for delivering a baby. The church also advocates the obeying of laws regarding immunizations and other health matters. God's goodness heals. They use scientific mental healing. *I guess there are limits to His powers; He doesn't handle straightening teeth or correcting faulty vision.*

Jehovah's Witness

This Christian sect was founded in the United States in the nineteenth century. They strongly believe the second coming of Christ will be in the near future. After the battle of Armageddon, the place where the final battle between good and evil will be fought, Christ will reign on Earth for a thousand years. Only a faithful few will be saved and of course, if you are a Jehovah's Witness you will be one of the saved. *More absolute thinking. At least these absolute thinkers are pacifist.* They preach door to door, trying to save others. They have strict rules based on their interpretation of the Bible. They do not celebrate birthdays or holidays, they are pacifist, they will not take part in politics and they will not accept blood transfusions. Jehovah is the name for God in the Old Testament. Jehovah's Witnesses do not meet in churches but kingdom halls and actually are opposed to Christian churches. *Now, be honest, who has pretended they are not home and not answered the door when they are in the neighborhood?*

Seventh-Day Adventist

This religion began in Massachusetts in 1831. They anticipate the second coming of Christ. Sabbath is on Saturday for Seventh-Day Adventists. There is great importance put on honoring the Bible.

They strongly advocate vegetarianism. The Bible tells us to be compassionate to all God's creatures, not kill them and eat them. Seventh-Day Adventists do not smoke or drink. William Miller, the founder, set a date for the second coming; it did not happen so he set another; it did not happen either. Adventists were disappointed. *But He is coming...soon.*

Quakers

The Society of Friends that "Quakes at the Word of the Lord." Quakers have no priests or rituals, they have meeting houses. They gather weekly for a prayer meeting where they pray silently together. Quakers do a lot of charity work. Quakers reject the necessity for ordained ministers; no go-between is needed. In the 1780s, it was the Quakers who started the Underground Railroad.

Salvation Army

William and Mary Booth founded this religion in 1865. The founders felt that the working class was not responding well to established Christian churches, so they started the Salvation Army. Repenting for sins and doing a lot of charity work, including providing food and shelter for the homeless, are important to the Salvation Army. *I honestly had no idea that this was a church.*

Amish

We all know the Amish because they reject technological advances and limit contact with the outside world. They even refuse to have cars. They still use horses and buggies. The Amish stress humility, family and community. They wear plain clothes. It is felt that plain clothes encourage humility and separation from the outside world.

Church of Christ

This church was founded in the United States of America. They believe in strictly following the teachings of the New Testament and reject all other traditions. The followers of this religion strive to be similar to each other, similar to the disciples of Jesus Christ.

Shakers

The Shaking Quakers. All believers are celibate, so new converts are relied upon to keep the religion going. *What?* I don't think it is going so well. No growth. The Shakers are splintered off from a Quaker community. Ann Lee started the Shakers in 1772. They strive for simplicity in daily lives. There is gender equality among Shakers. All individuality is suppressed. Simplicity in dress, food and living arrangements are ways to suppress individuality. They call themselves the United Society of Believers. They are known for their furniture which they sell to the outside world.

Somewhere there is a line between Christian and non-Christian. I am not quite sure where it is. It is apparently different for each individual and each form of religion. It is a little zigzagging. To be honest, I'm not sure why a line is even needed. Apparently for some, calling themselves Christian and whether or not someone else is Christian is very important. I have even heard several people say that Catholics are not true Christians. How can a person say they are Christian and then talk about hate or judge others? Why does it matter who is a "true Christian" and who is not? Isn't Christianity supposed to be based on compassion? Where is that brotherly love? That is one of the things that bothers me about religion. Why would anyone want to force their beliefs on others? Or make the rules for a whole country based on their beliefs? This "I am right and everyone outside my church is wrong" mentality is nuts. People who think that way need to re-evaluate. Who decides who is Christian and who is not? Some churches say Jesus Christ needs to be accepted as the savior, some say the Bible must be believed literally, and some do not care about Jesus or the Bible. Who makes the rules? Why are there rules? Who cares?

World Church of the Creator

This is a non-Christian, non-profit religious organization. *At least they do not try and hide behind the forgiving, loving Christians.* The prime objective is the survival and expansion of the white race. As the Reverend Matt Hale, PM of World Church of the Creator, would say, "a commitment to a whiter and brighter world." *Sounds like a sane man.* They see themselves as being motivated by a love of the white race and an extreme hatred for non-whites. This religion is based on white supremacy and racial hatred.

New Agers

New Agers feel that Jesus Christ was just one of a line of spiritual leaders that continues today. This religion is really a combination of many ancient religious traditions and a mixture of many current religious traditions with a little non-religious stuff thrown in the mix. New Agers feel God is us and we are God. This religion is centered on the self; all you need is within yourself.

Baha'i

People of the Baha'i faith believe that Judaism, Islam, Buddhism, Hinduism and Christianity all agree on the basic principles; the differences are unimportant details. This religion originated in Iran in the 1800s, so it is a fairly new religion, with roots in Islam. Baha'u'llah was the last in a line of prophets, some of which were Moses, Buddha, Jesus and Mohammed. They believe in one God. They want to end prejudice since we are all from a single race. They also want to gain equality for men and women. An individual has a responsibility to seek the truth. There is harmony between science and religion. An international government, a single language, eliminating all prejudice, and the importance of a universal education are some of the things that followers of the Baha'i religion are trying to achieve. They want to eliminate the negative effects of economic inequality. *Some of these things are good, but there will never be a single language and an international government.* They also stress the necessity of avoiding forbidden activities such as killing, stealing, lying, sexual misconduct, gambling, abusing drugs, abusing alcohol, and participating in malicious gossip.

Freemason

Freemasons feel that Jesus was not the Son of God and the Bible is not the will of God. It is a fraternal organization with strong moral values. The Freemasons have no theological doctrines, no sacraments and do not claim to lead its followers into salvation. They believe in a Supreme Being. Freemasons have three main duties: first, a duty to God; second, an obligation to family; third, a duty to help neighbors through charity and service. Mutual assistance and the promotion of brotherly love are the fundamental for this religion.

Unification Church

The Moonies. The official name is The Holy Spirit Association for the Unification of World Christians. Founder Sun Myung Moon claims to be the Messiah. The females who joined this church were required to have sex with Sun Myung Moon to cleanse them of Satan. *I wonder if you got to see a picture of Reverend Moon before you signed up.* The Reverend went back to Korea.

Wicca

Witchcraft and neo-pagan practitioners of the earth religions are forms of Wicca. They recognize the divinity of nature and of all living things, a harmony with all of life. The Earth Mother is worshipped and she is the creator of life. Wiccans worship nature, the seasons, the sun and the moon. The Church of All Worlds was the first pagan church, founded in 1968 by Oberon Zell-Ravenheart and recognized by the Internal Revenue Service in 1970. Wicca is a highly individual religion. There is no devil worship. There is no Bible. Groups of men and women meet on the new and full moons at festival times to raise energy and put themselves in touch with natural forces. During these meetings they also honor old and new gods and goddesses. *There is no eating of children. There is no Nimbus 2000s. For non-Harry Potter readers, that is a broom that witches and wizards fly on. No brooms at all in Wicca. Very different from what we think we know about witchcraft; it is very peaceful and harmless.*

International Society for Krishna Consciousness

Hare Krishna, Hare Krishna, Hare Krishna…ISKCON was founded in 1966. Krishna use the Bhagavad Gita (a Hindu text) as the central religious text. They reject the caste system. The main spiritual practice is chanting. Although the Bhagavad Gita is the main Hindu text, they are not Hindu. The Krishnas lead a simple life and are vegetarians.

Transcendental Meditation

The benefits of simple meditation techniques are used. Meditation is practiced twice a day for 12-20 minutes. The meditation techniques are based on Hindu philosophy. Transcendental Meditation was introduced to the West by Maharishi in 1959. It is a non-spiritual devotional practice that increases happiness, health, creativity, memory and energy.

Sikhism

In 1499 Guru Nanak said, "There is neither Muslim or Hindu, so whose path should I follow? I shall follow God's path." He meant that these outward differences between religions are unimportant in God's eye. Guru Nanak stressed the equality of everyone in God's eyes. Sikhs believe in one God, who should be worshipped by living honestly and caring for others. Sikhs cannot drink or smoke. They must work in a job that benefits society. Sikhs give 1/10 of their income to others. The scripture that the Sikh religion uses is called the *Guru Granth Sahib*. A Sikh temple is called a Gurdwara. A follower must cover the head, remove shoes and wash before entering the prayer room. Temples also serve as a place to sleep and a dining room for anyone who needs it. In the Sikh religion, there are no priests. Khalsa is the Sikh brotherhood. Women are included in the Khalsa. Hair goes uncut, so as to interfere as little as possible with nature. Turbans are worn to keep long hair neat. There are five rules for the Khalsa, or the five K's:

- Kachera—white shorts worn under clothing to symbolize purity and modesty
- Kara—a steel bangle worn on the right arm—a reminder to only fight for God
- Kangha—a wooden comb to keep hair clean and neat
- Kirpan—a short sword, a reminder to defend the truth and what is right; today, symbolic kirpan brooches are worn instead of real swords.
- Kesh—uncut hair, showing devotion to God

Islam

Islam means submission to God. Muslim means one who submits, therefore, a Muslim is a follower of the Islam faith. Islam is a monotheist religion. One God...Allah. Allah is all-seeing and all-powerful. There are two main types of Muslims, the Sunni sect, which includes about 90% of all Muslims, and the Shiite Muslims, who are a little more liberal. It is so important to gain a simple understanding, in the least, especially with all that is going on with the world. *Jihad* is translated as meaning "struggle," a struggle first and foremost with oneself to overcome lust, anger, greed and cynicism. The problems with terrorism are not with Muslims but they are with fundamentalists. People of the Middle East just take their religion very seriously; it is a way of life. Islam really does emphasize peace.

The Koran is the holy scripture of the Islamic religion, the final word of Allah. The Koran opens with "Praise to Allah." The Koran is extremely important to Muslims. Muslims believe that for the Koran to be authentic it must be in Arabic. The Koran has one hundred fourteen chapters. The chapters vary in length from 286 verses to a few lines. The Koran sets guidelines for relationships: people to people, people to God and people to all creation. Guidelines are also given for a just society. The Koran is a written record of the words revealed by Gabriel, the angel, from God to Mohammed. Many Muslims try to memorize all or parts of the Koran.

The Islam faith requires being devoted to Allah and practicing certain moral behaviors. Muslims have social and personal codes of conduct. Muslims demand good and reprimand evil. Muslims feel it is their religious duty to defend Allah, the Koran and their way of life. They do not gamble, drink alcohol, or eat pork. In Islam it is forbidden to kill animals just for the sport of it. Islam forbids attacks against non-combatants. It forbids the unnecessary destruction of property. *So 9/11 had absolutely nothing to do with Islam.* It is a peaceful religion.

SPIRITUAL CLARITY

Mohammed was the final and main prophet to Muslims. Jesus and Moses were also prophets; there were twenty-eight, ending with Mohammed. Mohammed was born in Mecca. When he was fourteen, in a cave near Mecca he received the first of many revelations from Allah. The angel Gabriel came before him and told him that he was a prophet. Muslims believe Jesus was only a man, not part of a trinity. Mohammed left Mecca for Medina. He lived in Medina until he died in 632 A.D.

Muslims, like Christians and Jews, believe that Abraham is the father of all. The Islamic faith did a lot for women's equality in the Islamic world. *You probably read that statement and thought I am crazy. You are thinking, "What about Afghanistan?" The Taliban was not Islam; they were fundamentalists, big difference. Al-Qaeda is not Islam.* Racial equality is also stressed, since everyone is a child of Allah. Justice requires that wrongdoers be punished. Muslims believe everyone is born with a clean sin slate. Sins can be overcome by acts of will. Muslims say Allah does not love those who do wrong; each person is responsible to earn salvation.

In Islam there will be a last day; the dead will be resurrected. Allah will be the judge and each person will be either sent to heaven or hell. Hell is for those who oppose Allah or his prophet, Mohammed.

Predestination is also an Islamic belief. Allah has determined what he pleases and no one can change what he has planned. From this doctrine comes a common Islamic phrase…"It is Allah's will."

Both men and woman of Islam dress modestly. There are no specific rules in Islamic scripture so "modesty" is interpreted differently. All meat must be prepared in a certain way to be edible. The name Allah must be uttered during slaughter and the blood, which is considered unclean, must be drained away. Alcohol consumption is not allowed because it can make people forget their duties to Allah.

A mosque is the official place for worship. Before entering a mosque, shoes must be removed. In a mosque, when praying you always face towards the *Qibla* wall, the wall that faces Mecca. Before praying *Wada* takes place. *Wada* is the ritualistic washing of the hands, face, mouth, and feet. Modesty is important in the Islamic faith, so women must cover their heads in a mosque.

The five pillars of Islam are:

- Shahadah—at no specific age, when a young Muslim is initiated into the faith. It is a confession of faith in Allah and his prophet, Mohammed. "There is no God but Allah and Mohammed is his messenger."
- Salat—ritual worship—five times a day—before sunrise, after midday, mid afternoon, shortly after sunset and in the fullness of the dark—facing Mecca—each worship time is about ten minutes.
- Siyaam—fasting during the holy month of Ramadan—no food, no drinking (even water), and no sex from sunrise to sunset. Doing this reminds the Muslims about the good things in life, and not to overindulge. It is a time for studying the Koran.
- Zakah—two and a half percent of all of a Muslim's wealth is given to the poor.
- Hajj—pilgrimage to Mecca, the central shrine in the Islamic faith. Everyone who can, must make this pilgrimage once in his or her lifetime. The poor, old, sick, and disabled do not have to go. Nobody is allowed to go without first making sure that their family is provided for in their absence.
- As-salamu alaikum—peace be to you—a popular greeting in Islam.

Islamic Holidays

- Ramadan—the whole ninth month of the Islamic calendar. It is a time of self-discipline, studying oneself, kindness and morality. The Koran is read completely during the month. Adults fast from sunrise to sunset the whole month. The month is set aside for reflection on past misdeeds and expressing gratitude to Allah.
- Lailut ul-Qadr—the last ten days of Ramadan. Muslims spend a lot of time in a mosque celebrating Mohammed's first divine revelation.

- Id ul-Adha—a time when animals are slaughtered to benefit the poor. It is a celebration of faithfulness.
- Al-Isra Wal Miraj—marks the journey Mohammed made from Mecca to Jerusalem to meet with Allah.

Jainism

Jainism is an Indian belief system: they share many beliefs with Hindus and Buddhists. Whenever I think of Jainism, I think of a picture in a comparative religion textbook from Drake University of a Jain monk walking down the street. He was wearing a mask, so as not to inadvertently breathe in any small flying insects, and sweeping so he would not step on any ants or other creepy crawlies.

This religion emphasizes charity and respect for all animal life. The *Acarangasutra* is the holy text for Jains. Followers of this religion are on a search for a way to release oneself from the cycle of existence, the cycle of birth and death. Jains have as few possessions as possible. Happiness does not come from material things.

Jains are strict vegetarians. They will not even eat root vegetables because the whole plant dies giving up its roots. Killing anything, including a plant, will have consequences, prolonging the cycle of life and death. Jains believe in the individual soul rather than a supreme being. The universe has no beginning and no end, therefore no creator.

Jains have five rules that they live by:

- Ahimsa—non-violence even when it comes to plants and animals
- Staya—speaking the truth
- Asteya—do not steal
- Brahma-charya—be sexually monogamous to one's spouse
- Aparigraha—be non-materialistic, detach from people, places and things

Zoroastrians

This religion was founded about 1800 B.C. in Persia, by the Zarathushtra. There is one God, Ahura Mazda. The emphasis in this religion is on the struggle between good and evil. Ahura Mazda is not to be feared but considered a friend. People are responsible for their own actions. Each individual is responsible for improving humanity. Zoroastrians pray five times a day. The objective is to live in harmony with nature. The religious motto is "Good thoughts. Good words. Good deeds." Decay and rust are to be avoided; purity is important. Death, bringing bodily decay along with it, is seen as a triumph of evil for a short period of time. The Earth must not be contaminated by the dead. Zoroastrians put the dead on "towers of silence" and let birds of prey consume the flesh, while they pray in a nearby building. The bones are later put in a pit.

Rastafarianism

Rastafarianism is fairly new; it was founded in the 1930s. It originated in Jamaica and is spreading to other Caribbean countries. They believe that a black messiah will be coming to Africa and to be truly free they must return to Africa. They stress a positive image of blackness and a message of freedom. Rastafarians live close to nature. They grow their own food. Many members of the religion are vegetarians. They do not drink alcohol or coffee. But they do use dry cannabis; they consider it a natural and beneficial herb; many smoke it as a part of worship.

Caodaism

Dao Cao Dai (Caodaism in English) is a religion centered in Vietnam. It combines elements from Buddhism, Confucianism, Christianity, Hinduism, Islam, Judaism, Taoism and Genissm, an indigenous religion of Vietnam.

Members of this religion believe in reincarnation. The cycle can be broken free of by cultivating self and finding God in self. Bad karma can cause reincarnation onto another planet where it is cold, dark, and miserable. Good karma leads to a happier next life. Karma determines one's future life by how things are practiced in this life. Really good karma could mean breaking the cycle.

Caodaism followers have a duty to themselves, their family, and society. Separation from material things is encouraged. Ancestors are worshipped. There are two sects in this religion:

- Exoterism—practice good and avoid evil, show kindness to humans, animals, plants and nature.
- Esoterism—practice meditation.

The five virtues are humility, obligation, civility, knowledge, and reliability.

Judaism

The covenant is an agreement that God made with Noah, Moses and Abraham. According to the Bible, God said he would establish a chosen people, a "great nation" from Abraham's descendants. These are the Jewish people, described in the Book of Genesis; in return Abraham and his followers would offer complete obedience to God.

Abraham's descendants moved to Egypt where they were taken as slaves by the Egyptians. After centuries of persecution the Hebrews were released from the pharaoh's rule and led by Moses to Canaan (Palestine). Hebrew is the sacred language of Judaism. The Jewish faith accepts Jesus, who was Jewish, as a good teacher or even a prophet but not the Messiah. On Mt. Sinai, God gave Moses the Ten Commandments to guide the conduct of God's people. The Ten Commandments serve as a moral code for Christianity and Judaism.

The Ten Commandments are located in Exodus 20:1-17, in the Bible. God spoke these words: "I am the Lord your God, who brought you out of Egypt, out of the land of slavery.
• You shall have no other Gods before me.
• You shall not make for yourself an idol in the form of anything in heaven above or on earth beneath or in the waters below. You shall not bow down to them or worship them; for I, the Lord your God, am a jealous God, punishing the children for the sin of the fathers to the third or fourth generation of those who hate me, but showing love to a thousand generations of those who love me and keep my commandments.
• You shall not misuse the name of the Lord your God, for the Lord will not hold anyone guiltless who misuses his name.
• Remember the Sabbath day by keeping it holy. Six days you shall labor and do all your work, but the seventh day is a Sabbath to the Lord your God. On it you shall not do any work, neither you, nor your son or daughter, nor your manservant or your maidservant, nor your animals, nor the alien within your gates. For in six days the Lord made the heavens and the earth, the sea, and all that is in them, but he rested on the seventh day. Therefore the Lord blessed the Sabbath day and made it holy.
• Honor your father and your mother, so that you may live long in the land the Lord your God is giving you.
• You shall not murder.
• You shall not commit adultery.
• You shall not steal.
• You shall not give false testimony against your neighbor.
• You shall not covet your neighbor's house. You shall not covet your neighbor's wife, or his manservant or maidservant, his ox or donkey, or anything that belongs to your neighbor."

The faith of Judaism is monotheistic. They believe that in return for love and obedience, God will sustain them as a people. In 1948, the United Nations declared Palestine the Jewish homeland. The state of Israel was born and became home to many Jews. Regarding sin, Judaism teaches that man is not born good or evil; he is born free to choose.

Important religious writings to Jews are the *Torah,* the first five books in the Old Testament of the Bible: Genesis, Exodus, Leviticus, Numbers, and Deuteronomy. Also the *Talmud* contains Jewish teachings. Orthodox Jews follow the *Mishnah,* which are instructions for daily living.

Orthodox Jews take a literal or fundamental approach to faith. They avoid change and are very traditional. They have as little contact as possible with the outside world. An example of an Orthodox Jew would be a man with those long sideburns because a part of the Old Testament says it is a sin to cut your sideburns. Conservative Jews realize that contact is inevitable in daily lives, but they try to keep ancient traditions alive. Reform Jews emphasize the moral lessons of the Jewish traditions, but try to be more liberal.

The spiritual leader of a Jewish congregation is called a rabbi. A synagogue is the Jewish place of worship. Liturgy is public worship or ritual. Group prayer is extremely important in the Jewish tradition. Women are only allowed to be rabbis in some of the Reform synagogues. One of the fundamentals of the Jewish religion is cleanliness. Since women menstruate, they are not considered as clean as men, therefore are not allowed to become rabbis in Orthodox or Conservative synagogues.

Jews practice cleanliness and the avoidance of unclean animals. Kosher is what food is called if it is prepared in a certain way. Meat must be from animals that chew a cud and have cloven hooves (sheep or cows). The animals are slaughtered a certain way and all traces of blood is removed to be kosher. Seafood and chicken are considered kosher if prepared in the same manner. No dairy products are consumed with and not immediately before or after meals that contain meat. Separate cooking and serving utensils are required for dairy and non-dairy foods.

Orthodox Jews even pray after a trip to the bathroom, thanking God for the amazing bodies we all have and what they do.

Jewish Holidays

• Rosh Hashanah—the Jewish New Year. Happens somewhere from mid-September to mid-October; celebrates the creation of the Earth as described in the book of Genesis.
• Yom Kippur—Day of Atonement, after Rosh Hashanah; sundown one day to sundown the next day, Jews do not work, do not drink anything, do not eat and repent for misdeeds of the past year.
• Sukkot—harvest celebration, lasts about eight days, is in late October, no work on the first and last days.
• Hanukkah—sometimes spelled Chanukah, the Festival of Lights, early to mid-December, lasts eight days, celebrates the struggle for religious freedom, commemorates the Maccabes victory over the Syrians. When the Maccabes (a small band of Jewish religious freedom fighters) reclaimed their temple, there was only enough oil left to burn for one night. It burned for eight days, until more oil could be obtained. Today Jewish people celebrate the holiday by lighting a candle for each of the eight days in a menorah.
• Purim—late in February or early March, celebrates the deliverance of Persian Jews from destruction, Book of Esther in the Bible, a day of fasting and joy.
• Passover—late March or early April. In the book of Exodus, God arranged for all of the first born Egyptians to be killed by the Angel of Death. The Angel of Death was told to "Passover" all of the marked houses with Jewish occupants.
• Shavout—celebrates the spring harvest and God's gift of the Torah.
• Brit milah—circumcision. In Genesis 17:10, God tells Abraham that all his male descendants should be circumcised

Another interesting fact is that Jews do not embalm their dead. Reform Jews will allow cremation but not other forms of Judaism.

Confucianism

Confucius was the supreme philosopher of ancient China. He placed more emphasis on ethical and political matters than religious doctrine. Although Confucius's focus was on moral behavior and social interactions, there is an important spiritual foundation to his teachings. The *Analects of Confucius* are considered to be the most accurate account of his teachings. The *Analects of Confucius* were not compiled by Confucius himself but by his followers. *I Ching*, or the *Book of Changes*, is also considered to be an inspired work to Confucians.

Analect 12.16 Confucius says "Judge not, so that you will not be judged." Sounds like the Bible, doesn't it?

Another says: "The gentleman calls attention to good points in others; he does not call attention to their defects. The small man does just the reverse of this."

Yin and yang are polar aspects of primal energy. The force that ties all humans to each other is Jen. Jen can also be described as compassion and love. Confucius taught that proper action comes from Li, correct etiquette and ritual.

Taoism

Taoism is "the way the universe works." The art of keeping it simple. Tao action is inaction, non-control and non-interference. Tao means "path or way." Taoists reject goal-oriented effort. They believe that Tao is everywhere at all times. Taoism and Confucianism are complimentary belief systems. Tao is creative and beyond literal expression. There is emphasis on the balance of nature. The *Tao Te Ching* is the central Taoist text. The *I Ching*, or

Book of Changes, is considered inspired work. Taoism and Confucianism have an intertwined history. Some important Tao principles are:

- As to dwelling—live near the ground
- As to thinking—hold to which is simple
- As to conflict—pursue fairness and generosity
- As to governance—do not attempt to control
- As to work—do what you like doing
- As to family—be fully present

Shinto

Shinto is the indigenous, nature focused religion of Japan. They place a great emphasis on tradition and ceremonial customs rather than formal religious doctrines. Shinto's origins date back to prehistory. *Kami* is the Shinto faith. Shinto has no founder and no written scriptures. It has no specific patterns for worship and no rules regarding Kami. Shinto is a form of nature worship. It does not promote a specific moral code. There is no supreme god. The sun goddess, Amaterasu, is important. The emperor of Japan is known as a direct descendant of Amaterasu. Ritual and tradition are essential to Shinto. Ritual and tradition are also important to the Japanese culture. Matsuris are festivals honoring the spirits.

Kami can be practiced at any place or time. Shrines are made of wood, near trees and flowing water. Shinto's many rituals celebrate purity, clarity and contact with the diverse forces. Many Shinto rituals are closely linked to the seasons, with planting and harvest times being important. Daily Shinto life is part of the Japanese culture.

New Shinto sects have developed that emphasize brotherhood and world peace.

Shinto core beliefs:

- Shinto places importance on the family unit.
- Tradition is important. Shinto celebrates major life events as marriage and birth; traditions are passed from generation to generation.
- Closeness to nature.
- Physical cleanliness.
- Festivals to honor spirits or a specific spirit.

Roma

Romas are also known as Rom, Gypsies, Rroma, and Romani. This group of people has suffered heavy persecution, from the witch-hunts to Hitler. One Christian ruler actually made a law giving Christians permission to kill Romas. In 1721, Emperor Karl VI, of what is now Germany, ordered the total genocide of the Roma. "Gypsy hunts" were organized to track down Romas and kill them. Romas believe in the existence of God (Del), the existence of Satan (Beng), the existence of bad luck (bibaxt), the existence of ghosts (mulo), the power of good luck charms, the power of amulets, the power of talisman, the powers of curses, and the power of healing ritual.

When a Roma dies, people gather to ask forgiveness. They are extremely superstitious. They even plug the nose of the dead with wax to prevent evil spirits from entering the dead body.

Women are considered dirty. *What is this with women being dirty? I shower every morning.* Women cannot shave their legs. Men's and women's clothes are washed separately to avoid contamination. If a woman is menstruating or is pregnant than she is really dirty. She needs to go down river to wash her clothes so as not to spread the dirt around.

Babies are baptized. Children are married between the ages of nine and fourteen. This tradition is changing, due to the outside influences. *I cannot imagine children at this age caring for a family.*

In 1997 the first Roma/Christian Church opened in Los Angeles, California. Since then fifty more have opened across the United States. Some Roma women tell fortunes for non-Romas for money.

Vodun

Vodun is also known as Vodou, Voodoo, Sevi and LWA. It is most commonly called Voodoo. In 1996 Voodoo became the official religion of Benin, a republic in Africa. Many adults in Haiti follow the Vodun religion. It can also be found in many large cities of North America and many similar religions can be found in South America.

Voduns believe in a supreme being. The main God is Olorun, who is distant and unapproachable. A lesser god, Obatala, was responsible for creating the Earth and life. There are hundreds of minor spirits. Loa are similar to Christian saints, since they are people held in special regard and because they led exceptional lives. Houngans are male priests and mambo are female priests.

Many rituals are held. The purpose of a ritual is to make contact with a spirit and please the spirit by offering either animal sacrifices or gifts. Rituals also celebrate seasonal or momentous occasions like healing, birth, marriage and death. These ceremonies consist of feasts, chanting, beating purified drums, shaking purified rattles, dancing and animal sacrifice. Vodun believers truly feel that zombies exist. Zombies are the dead who are brought back after burial. A zombie has no will of its own but is under the control of an evil sorcerer who administers powerful drugs to keep the zombie alive. *Hmm...*

Buddhism

Buddhism developed in India. It shares with Hinduism the concept of Karma (what you do in this life affecting what you do in the next. When I think of Karma I think of an episode of *Friends*. Chandler did something awful and asks for Phoebe's advice. Phoebe believes in Karma. She tells him that in his next life, he will now come back as a dung beetle), reincarnation and the goal of entering Nirvana. Nirvana is the final state of liberation from the cycle of life and death...total enlightenment. Buddhists seek to escape lustful desires by self-effort. Practices and beliefs are derived from the teachings of Siddharta Gautama (the Buddha or the Enlightened One).

About 6th century B.C., Siddharta Gautama was an Indian prince who attained enlightenment after decades of seeking, fasting and meditation. One day he sat under a tree, not getting up for eight days until he attained enlightenment. He taught that all desires lead to suffering, which can be overcome by self-discipline. Siddharta became the Buddha.

The Four Noble Truths of Buddhism are:

- Life is suffering.
- Suffering is caused by desire.
- Desire can be overcome.
- The Eightfold Path can overcome desire.

The Eightfold Path is:

- The right viewpoint—understanding the Four Noble Truths.
- The right values—consideration and compassion rather than selfishness and competitiveness.
- The right speech—avoid anger, aggression, exaggeration, lies and gossip.
- The right actions—living honestly and not harming other living things; many Buddhists are vegetarians.
- The right livelihood—avoiding jobs which harm others, no drug dealers or weapons dealers.
- The right effort—thinking good thoughts to have a healthy mind.
- The right mindfulness—practicing calming the mind so it can be free of distractions.

• The right concentration—meditate to lead to nirvana and enlightenment.

How can you go wrong, living this way? This makes perfect sense. *Living Buddha, Living Christ* by Thich Nhat Hanh says that you can believe in God while practicing Buddhist principles.

There are five main branches of Buddhism: Mahayanna, Theravada, Vajrayana, Pure Land, and Zen Buddhism. Buddha taught that one should not seek divine intervention in his or her life. Hindu gods and other gods do exist but they do not hold domain over daily life. Buddha's path focuses on individual pursuit of spiritual goals. A two-year-old farm family's child was recognized as a reincarnation of the thirteenth Dalai Lama; he was brought to Tibet and trained to become Tenzin Gyatso, the fourteenth Dalai Lama. The Dalai Lama is the spiritual leader of Tibet. Tibet is essentially Buddhist headquarters, although the Dalai Lama is currently exiled. His holiness is in India since he was forced out of Tibet by the Chinese government. Tibet wants to be a country by itself and China will not let it; the Dalai Lama was getting in the way.

Buddhist Holidays

• Nirvana Day—February 15, celebrates Buddha's passing.
• Buddha Day—April 8, celebrates Buddha's birth.
• Bodhai Day—December 8, the day Prince Gatauma sat under the Bodhi tree vowing to remain there until he attained supreme enlightenment.

African Religions

Most African cultures consider religion to be an important part of life. The different areas in Africa have creation stories that tie the people in that area to the gods they worship. Religious traditions are passed down orally by parents or priests.

Most African religions believe in sacred places. Religious leaders feel it is their duty to preserve their culture from the outside world. The ultimate goal is to prepare for death and afterlife. There are many rituals to aid in this preparation. Rituals celebrate birth, puberty, initiation to adulthood, marriage, having children, death and afterlife. The rituals let people know what is expected of them in this life and the next.

Hinduism

Hinduism is the native religion of India. There is no organized belief system in Hinduism, it is very diverse. Hindus follow no specific doctrine. It encompasses various practices and beliefs recognized for centuries by millions. Hinduism has no founder; believers feel it has existed forever. Hinduism is a complex religion that can answer questions about how to achieve whatever the follower wants.

Hindus do not believe in a personal loving god, but in Brahma, a formless, abstract being, who is the beginning of all things. Some Hindus believe in one god, some believe in many gods and still others do not believe in any gods. There is a basic group of three main Gods, a trinity of sorts: Brahma, the creator; Vishnu, the sustainer; and Shiva, the destroyer. Hinduism is hard to sum up in a couple paragraphs. It is difficult to understand.

Here is a little more to add to the confusion:

- Brahma—a specific creator God, one of the supreme deities.
- Brahman—Hindu term for ultimate reality, eternity, supreme being.
- Brahmin—a priestly caste member.

The caste system is the social hierarchy of India and Hinduism. *The Vedas* are ancient writings important to Hinduism. The Brahmin are the only ones allowed to read *The Vedas.* These ancient writings include hymns to Hindu gods and thoughts about existence. The

Bhagavad Gita is the main Hindu text. It stresses union with Brahma can be achieved through love, compassion, and complete devotion. Brahma or the absolute truth can be reached in many ways.

Hindus call their sin "utter illusion," because they believe reality is an illusion. The physical world is not real. They seek deliverance from Samsara, the cycle of reincarnation. Reincarnation is when one is trapped in the cycle of life and death until union with Brahma is achieved, only then can Nirvana (true enlightenment or heaven) be reached. Karma is when your next life will be determined by your actions in this life. Karma holds believers accountable for their actions. Hardships are caused by bad actions in a previous life. Dharma is the code of behavior, which governs all aspects of life.

Animals are treated well in Hindu societies. Peacocks and cattle are sacred; their slaughter is not permitted for any reason.

Santeria

Santeria is a combination of Caribbean religious customs and Roman Catholicism. Regla de Ocha is the proper name for this religion. Santeria (the way of the saints) is a more common name. It dates back to when slaves from Africa were brought to the Caribbean and forced into the Catholic religion. African beliefs and Catholic beliefs combined to form Santeria. Many gods from the old, suppressed beliefs were kept alive by becoming Catholic saints. Santeria has followers in Cuba, Caribbean islands, Puerto Rico, parts of the United States, South America, France and the Netherlands.

Olrun is the supreme deity and the creator. Orishas are the deities associated with Catholic saints. The Orishas need animal sacrifice, prepared dishes and human praise to stay effective. Sacrifice is an important part of the ritual. Sacrifice brings food luck, purification, and the forgiveness of sins.

At the ritual, dancing and rhythmic sounds supposedly lead to an individual being possessed by an Orisha. The individual then speaks and acts as the Orisha. Much of Santeria practice is kept secret. To learn more about Santeria, you must convert. Santeria has no religious text.

Native American Spirituality

Followers of Native American spirituality do not treat their spiritual beliefs and practices as "religion" the same way that Christians do. Beliefs and practices are a way of life, part of their very being.

Different areas have varying beliefs stemming from the ways of gathering food and living in separate regions. There are countless indigenous religions. There is no official scripture. These religions place a heavy emphasis on nature. The shaman or medicine man is a religious celebrant, who is considered to have powers, the ability to understand and treat diseases.

These religions usually have a main god, a source of all, who is ever present, universal, a sustainer, and the one who determines destinies. There are other spirits and ancestors operating under the main god. These beliefs share a profound and powerful spiritual connection to the natural world and their land.

Certain Indian tribes do not believe in heaven or hell. The reward for living a good life is…a good life. *Nothing mystifying here—this makes sense. They had something; maybe we should have converted instead of trying to get them to become Christians.*

Satanism

Satanists do not worship the devil. They do not worship a living deity either. Heaven and hell do not exist. Satan is not a living entity; he is a force of nature. Satanism respects life. Animals and children are not abused or killed. Emphasis is placed on the power and authority of the individual Satanist. They believe that each person is responsible for their own life. The highest of all satanic holidays is the birthdays of the followers.

The Church of Satan was founded in 1966 by Anton Szandor LaVey. There is a Satanic Bible; it was written in 1969. The Church of Satan is highly decentralized, believing that a strong central organization is not a good thing, especially since each Satanist is expected to follow his or her own path. Satanists do have some rules for behavior including, not killing humans or animals in rituals, not committing suicide, do unto others as they do unto you and to indulge oneself in the seven deadly sins. The seven deadly sins are greed, gluttony, pride, envy, anger, lust and sloth.

Membership in the Church of Satan is limited to adults of legal age, unless a teenager gets written permission from a parent or legal guardian. *Not good, but definitely not as bad as you thought, is it?*

Kabbalah

Kabbalah is a mystical form of Judaism. Kabbalists feel God does not command, dictate, reward or punish. The main principle in Kabbalah is: Love thy neighbor as thyself. All the rest is mere commentary. Now go and learn.

The major text of Kabbalah is called the *Zohar*. Guess who authored the first written work on Kabbalah...Abraham! He wrote that four thousand years ago. A Kabbalah religious leader is a rabbi. Kabbalah can answer the questions that most ask like, why is life filled with so much pain and confusion? Why are we here? How can I achieve constant fulfillment in my life? Kabbalists feel the Bible is a code that needs to be deciphered. It takes a much deeper understanding than a simple literal interpretation.

The following quote was at the beginning of Yehunda Berg's book *The Power of Kabbalah*:

In seeking wisdom, the first stage is silence, the second listening, the third remembrance, the fourth practice, the fifth teaching.

-Kabbalist Solomon Gabirol, c. 1045

Bibliography

Frederick, Shun; World religions, Religion, History & Literature http://www.geocities.com/Athens/Forum?1699/, America Online

Berg, Marcus J.; *Reading the Bible Again for the First Time.* San Francisco, CA: HarperCollins Publishers, Incorporated, 2001

Finkelstein, Israel & Silberman, Neil Asher; *The Bible Unleashed,* New York, NY: The Free Press: A Division of Simon & Schuster, Incorporated, 2001

Yancey, Phillip; *Reaching for the Invisible God*, Grand Rapids, MI: Zondervan, 2000

Ridnour, Fritz; *So What's the Difference,* Ventura, CA: Regal Books, 2000

Stevenson, Ph.D., Jay; *The Complete Idiot's Guide to Eastern Philosophy*, Indianapolis, IN; Alpha Books, 2000

Santeria, a Syncretistic Caribbean Religion, http://www.religioustolerance.org/santeri.htm

Kreeft, Peter & Tacelli, Ronald K.; *Handbook of Christian Apologetics*, Downers Grove, IL; InterVarsity Press, 1970

Meredith, Susan; *The Usborne Book of World Religions*, Tulsa, OK: Usborne Printing, 1995

Toropov, Brandon & Father Lee Buckles; *The Complete Idiot's Guide to World Religions,* New York, NY: Alpha Books, 1997

Russell, Bertrand; *Religion & Science*, Oxford, United Kingdom: Oxford University Press, 1997

McLennan, Reverend Scotty; *Finding Your Religion*, San Francisco, CA: Harper Collins, 1999

His Holiness the Dalai Lama, *Live in a Better Way*, Hamondworth, Middlesex, England: Penguin Congress, 1999

Caodiasm, http://www.religioustolerance.org/caodiasm.htm, America Online

Vodun, http://www.religioustolerance.org/voodoo.htm, America Online

About the Church of Satan, http://www.religioustolerance.org.satanis1.htm, America Online

World Church of the Creator, http://www.religioustolerance.org/wcotc.htm, America Online

Native American Spirituality, http://religioustolerance.org.ntaspir.htm, America Online

Covenant of the Goddess: About Witchcraft, http://www.org/general/iabout.html, America Online

Berg, Yehunda; *The Power of Kabbalah*; Jodere Group, Inc.; San Diego, CA; 2001

Grimbol, Pastor William R.; *The Complete Idiot's Guide to the Life of Christ*; Pearson Education In.; 2000

Krakauer, Jon; *Under the Banner of Heaven*; Doubleday; United States of America; 2003

Evolution and Common Sense

The further the spiritual evolution of mankind advances, the more certain it seems to me that the path to genuine religiosity does not lie through the fear of life, and the fear of death, and blind faith, but through striving after rational knowledge.
-Albert Einstein

Light will be thrown on the origin of man and his history.
-Charles Darwin, *The Origin of Species*

Evolution is clever than you are.
-Orgel's Second Rule

Nature herself has imprinted on the minds of all, the idea of God.
-Cicero

All questions about life have the same answer: Natural Selection.
-Henry Bennet-Clark

Providing that one has the courage to ask questions, to be dissatisfied, to think with the mind and heart one actually has, and not with the mind and heart one is supposed to have.
-Karl Rahner, S.J.

You cannot convince a believer of anything; for their belief is not based on evidence, but it is based on a deep-seated need to believe.
-Carl Sagan

If we are going to teach creation science as an alternative to evolution then we should also teach the stork theory as an alternative to biological reproduction.

-Judith Hayes, *The Happy Heretic*

The Facts

The study of evolution puts into perspective our relative insignificant existence and our enormous impact on the Earth. People who deny evolution must have a hard time swallowing the fact that humans are just a teeny tiny portion of what there is in the 13.7 billion-year-old universe. We are a microscopic speck. They seem to like the theory with the humans being the center of the universe or at least the geocentric theory with the Earth being the center. No wonder they had a hard time accepting the Copernican theory. The Copernican theory or the heliocentric theory declared that the Earth revolved around the sun, therefore the sun is the center of the universe not the Earth. Literal interpretation of the story of creation from the beginning of the Bible goes right along with the flat Earth method of thinking.

Whether it was the Big Bang or God snapping his fingers, the earth is 4.5 billion years old. The entire universe has been dated with precision at the ripe old age of 13.7 billion years old. The age of the Earth is not a guess based on the age of a few rocks; over the last thirty years many laboratories all over the world have come to the same conclusion.

Age is determined by combining absolute dating (calculating radioactive decay) and relative dating. Relative dating is determining age by observing what rock strata lie above and below. Strata are the specific layers of rock in a formation. Rocks are in certain layers and so are fossils. The deeper you dig, the more primitive the fossils are. Stratiography is the study of the layers of the Earth's surface. The study of stratiography is a way to understand the history of life on Earth.

Creationists argue that you cannot achieve order from chaos. The comparison of evolution to standing on a chair and dropping a deck of cards was actually given to me. What does 52-card pick up have anything to do with the world evolving? I can just see some preacher doing this and his congregation gasping at the delusional realization that evolution was just plain wrong. The answer to the argument that you cannot achieve order from chaos is that you can, if you add a little energy. An example would be cleaning your garage (chaos) x you cleaning it (energy) = a clean garage (order). Throwing the deck of cards on the floor and then picking them up would create order. Just add a little energy and things start to happen. The sun provides our world with a constant source of energy. The sun makes plants grow and become edible. Animals eat those plants. Other animals eat the animals that ate the plants. Life goes on and is constantly evolving.

A short time ago it was commonly believed the universe was only 6,000-10,000 years old. Unrealistic creationists actually still believe this. By the 19th century, with the new science of geology, we now know for certain that the Earth is closer to being 4.5 billion years old. Creationists interpret the Bible's story of creation literally. They believe that the universe and all that is in it have been created by divine intervention. Basically, it is a refusal to see facts. How can anyone with any sense dispute evolution?

Radioactive Aging

Radiocarbon dating was first developed in 1947. It is used to determine the approximate ages of dead organisms, artifacts, rock formations, and so on, by measuring the amount of Carbon-14 they contain. The method is possible because Carbon-14 is an isotope. An isotope (try to remember high school chemistry class) is an atom with a differing number of protons and neutrons, so it is unstable. Each atom has protons and neutrons in the center with electrons orbiting the outside. Isotope's half-lives are the time it takes for one-half of the radioactive material to decay. Carbon-14's half-life is 5,730 years. It takes another half-life for the next half of Carbon-14 to disintegrate and so on.

All living organisms absorb Carbon-14 during their lifetime by breathing and eating. After an organism dies and becomes a fossil, Carbon-14 continues to decay without being replaced. To measure how much Carbon-14 is left in a fossil, scientists burn a small piece. Radiation counters are used to detect the electrons given off by decaying Carbon-14 as it turns into nitrogen. The amount of Carbon-14 is compared to the amount of a stable form of carbon, to determine how much radiocarbon has decayed and to date the fossil.

In one creationist attack on carbon dating it was said that carbon dating is misunderstood, therefore faulty. Everyone thinks that carbon dating works for millions and billions of years. It does not, so it must not work. That argument is misleading, as most religious propaganda tries to brainwash or coerce people into believing the creationist version by using twisted half-truths. Using Carbon-14 dating, things can only be dated to about 23,000 years old. The information that is conveniently not mentioned is that other isotopes that decay at a much slower rate are used to date things older than 23,000 years. Carbon-14 is not the only radioactive isotope used for dating older objects.

Each rock has several isotopes; the specific half-life of these isotopes dates the rock. Here are a few, I am including them just to clarify that there are many methods for radioisotope dating. Potassium-40 is another radioactive element naturally found in your body and its half-life is 1.3 billion years. Uranium-235 has a half-life of 704 million years. Uranium-238 has a half life of 4.5 billion years. Thorium-232 has a half-life of 14 billion years. Rubidium-87 has a half-life of 49 billion years. The point, once again, is that there are a lot more isotopes used for dating other than Carbon-14. The use of various radioisotopes allows the dating of biological and geological samples with a high degree of accuracy. The actual definition for radioactive dating is "the determination of the age of an object or material based on the known rates of decay of radioactive isotopes of various elements."

Pangaea

In 1912, the German scientist Alfred Wegner proposed a theory that all present-day continents once made up a single land mass or super continent. That super continent is called Pangaea. The name Pangaea means "all lands" in Greek. Pangaea began to break apart in stages and drifted away from each other, eventually landing where they are now. This break up took place in the Mesozoic era. This is the theory of continental drift.

Wegner researched and used the evidence he found to support his theory. The similarities in the West African coastline and the coastline of eastern South America matched perfectly. Fossils of animals and plants were the same on opposite sides of the ocean. After gathering information to support his theory, he wrote *The Origin of Continents and Oceans*.

Further evidence that supports this theory besides the already stated is all the continents seemed to fit together like a giant puzzle. There is a distinctive rock stratum that is identical on opposite sides of the ocean. Also, coal is found underground in dry, cold Antarctica. Coal needs wet, warm regions to form. How can these things be explained without Pangaea?

Life

The earliest fossilized form of life was living about 3.5 billion years ago. At this point all of life consisted of microorganisms and algae. Now for a fossil to even form is a rare occurrence. Conditions must be just right for a soft-tissue body to get through not decomposing or being eaten by other animals or some other natural occurrence that would destroy the skeletal system. Only a microscopic portion of the organisms that have died even make it to the fossil stage. Only a small portion of the small portion of fossils that formed actually get discovered and studied.

The oldest fossil of a multi-cellular organism was found in Michigan and is reported to be 2.1 billion years old. About 600 million years ago aquatic worms appeared. About 400 million years ago the first vertebrates showed up. All life at that time was in the water. *Rhipidistians* were primitive fish with muscular lobes for fins. These fish had the ability to shuffle on land. They came out of the water during droughts to move to another area where water was available. Basically, these were gill breathers with the ability to gulp air and then extract the needed oxygen from the air. These fish were able to survive by getting from one drying water hole to the next water hole. As the droughts became more severe, natural selection favored the animals that could survive out of the water. These fish became our first reptiles.

Finally, about 200 million years ago, mammals evolved. So basically we all share the common ancestor not of primates but a shrew-like mammal that lived about 150-200 million years ago. We could trace our family tree back many more generations to an aquatic worm being a relative from long before or even further to a microorganism living in the water.

The Mesozoic time period is also known as the "Age of Reptiles." The first known mammals and birds split away from the dinosaurs. The dinosaurs had a two hundred year reign. What happened 65 million years ago? We probably will never know for sure. We have proof that they existed and ceased to exist 65 million years ago, not six thousand years ago.

Jerry Seinfeld, in his hilarious 1993 book, *SeinLanguage,* talked about the possibility of finding out what happened to the dinosaurs and compared it to the Kennedy assassination, which we could not solve with films. How could we possibly figure out why dinosaurs disappeared that long ago?

The first bird, *Archaepterx*, is clearly a descendant from reptiles. Then came the mammals. Tim M. Berra, who wrote *Evolution and the Myth of Creationism*, states that primates, the mammalian order to which we belong, arose and were widespread by about 38 million years ago.

Our Direct Ancestors

Australopithecines, which emerged about 4 or 5 million years ago, are sometimes called "Ape-man" or "missing link" because they are one of the many transitions between ape and man. They were the first upright walkers. The fossil of the hip and knee joints tell us this. Perhaps they started walking to carry helpless infants. Infants of species with larger brains are more helpless at birth because they physically could not be born with heads large enough to hold that big of a brain, so to compensate the brain develops outside the mother. Donald Johanson found the first transitional fossil with an ape-like head on an upright body. This fossilized skeleton was *Australopithecus afarensis*, or Lucy. Since this first find, many more transitional fossils have been found.

Cro-Magnon man is not really a separate scientific classification. Cro-Magnon is merely a group of *Homo sapiens* living 10 to 30 thousand years ago in Europe. In 1868, in the village of Les Eyzies in France, a group of skeletons were discovered. They were called Cro-Magnons.

A brief rundown of the development of man is:

- First we had different forms *of Australopithecus*.
- They developed into a couple forms with only *Homo habilis* emerging.
- *Homo habilis* became *Homo erectus*.
- *Homo erectus* became *Homo sapiens* and Neanderthal man; only *Homo sapiens* developed.
- *Homo sapiens* is now us…human beings in 2005.

If primates are not our direct ancestors, than why do you suppose that we share 98% of our genetic makeup with them?

Homo sapiens

There were a few frauds and mistakes (like Piltdown Man and Nebraska Man) and evolutionary dead ends in our study of what leads up to *Homo sapiens*. We are beginning to get the picture and have a lot more that is yet to be learned.

The first time the *Homo* species appeared was as *Homo habilis*. *Homo habilis* was known as "handy man" because of tools found with his fossils. *Homo habilis* was the first to leave Africa. Africa seems to be where man originated. During the whole time that *Homo habilis* existed, his brain size continued to grow.

Homo erectus continued to migrate away from Africa. His brain was larger than *Homo habilis*. *Homo erectus* was the first to use fire. The use of fire would change life considerably; he could now see in the dark; he could scare predators away; it would make it easier to keep warm and food could now be cooked. I would think that cooked meat would taste considerably better than raw meat. Peking Man, Turkana Child and Java Man were all *Homo erectus*.

At the point were the family tree split into Neanderthal man and *Homo sapiens*; they actually co-existed for awhile. Any readers of Jean Auel's Clan of the Cave Bear series (which are great!) already know this. Approximately 40,000 to 100,000 years ago these two species came into contact with one another. They had comparable brain size. Neanderthals have been discovered with evidence of ceremonial burials. They obviously believed in the afterlife. *Homo sapiens neanderthal* had a more muscular build and was stronger than *Homo sapiens*. To see what *Homo sapiens* looked like, just go look at yourself in the mirror.

The reason that *Homo sapiens* made it and *Homo sapiens neanderthal* did not is probably that *Homo sapiens* were just more able to adapt than Neanderthal man. You have got to go with the flow. *Homo sapiens neanderthal* did not and therefore became extinct.

Now after reading about all the types and succession of early man, how can anyone say there are no transitional fossils? The statement, which I encountered, "There are no transitional fossils" is just more creationist imbecility. They are all transitional fossils!

Genetics

Nancy Gibbs wrote a recent article for *Time* magazine entitled "The Secret of Life." Some of her points were: James Watson and Francis Crick did not discover the existence of DNA, they discovered its structure. A strip of DNA contains a code written in words of four chemical letters: A, T, G, and C. Uncoiled and stretched out, it would be six feet long; folded back up, it would be small enough to fit into one of our cells. DNA carries within it instructions for making a human. The instructions are similar for everything that lives; we are the cousins to the trees and insects. Some of these genes trace back to a time when we were fish. More than 200 come directly from bacteria. Our DNA provides a history book of where we came from and how we evolved. Every human being on the planet is 99.9% the same.

Evolution makes more sense with a basic knowledge of genetics. Chromosomes carry the genes which carry the DNA. DNA is in genes, which are on the chromosomes that are in every cell in the human body. Human DNA is basically the blueprint for a human being, including all behaviors and traits. Essentially building blocks for making a human being.

Alleles are different forms of the same gene contributed to the offspring of each parent. Parents only transmit half their genes to each offspring. These genes are in different combination in every sibling, except in the case of identical twins.

A mutation is any alteration of genetic information. Mutations occur when any change is made in DNA. Change a T to a G in a strand of DNA or change the length of a strand of DNA and abnormal biochemical reactions start happening. A delicate system can be easily thrown out of whack. Any change in these complex instructions can cause many problems: cancer, digestive tract disease, hereditary spastic paraplegia, multiple sclerosis, Parkinson's disease, heart disease, Alzheimer's disease, emotional problems and many more problems. Mutations can also be beneficial; they can help an organism adapt more easily to their environment.

Gradualism

There is constant variation in characteristics of a species and more variation with each generation. Evolution is a change in a gene pool of a population over time. This is gradualism…slow evolution; each change could take tens of thousands of years. One pro-creation argument I encountered was that since evolution cannot be witnessed it must be false. Has God been witnessed? Was creation witnessed?

This argument makes no sense. Another argument was that if evolution was true than we would have more than two arms to get more things done. What? When hearing these arguments it becomes obvious that the speakers are ignorant. When will people learn that if they are not informed maybe they should be quiet? Gradualism is the key word here. We are a very young species...only 50,000 years old, so do not expect to see any change during your lifetime. GRADUALISM! I really have a hard time understanding why this concept is so hard to grasp.

Evolution in Action

Evolution is the gradual adaptation of organisms to their environment through positive mutations. Organisms displaying characteristics which enable them to better adapt to their environment are more likely to reproduce and hence to produce more offspring, causing a gradual shift in the gene pool. These changes, if large enough, can eventually start a new species. This concept is "survival of the fittest."

Darwin

Charles Darwin is the name tied to evolution. He thought evolution was a series of gradual transformations, much too gradual to be observed in our lifetime. As Patrick Tort discussed in his informative book, *Darwin and the Science of Evolution*, the fact that gradualism was what Charles Darwin thought of as the basis of evolution—mutations occur continuously and imperceptible at times to create changes slowly over time.

From 1831-1836 Charles Darwin sailed on the *Beagle* and studied the influence climate and the environment had on living creatures. Darwin traveled on the *Beagle* from Europe to Cape Verde, around South America, to the Galapagos Islands to Tahiti, to Australia, around Africa and back to Europe. My point being he had substantial evidence to back his theories. He made many additional stops on his journey where he observed the geographic distribution, the similarities of living and extinct species living in the same area. He also studied how the species of man can affect nature. In Darwin's travels, another area of interest to him was differences in human culture. He criticized the practice of slavery which the Bible approves of.

After his trip Charles Darwin gathered enough information to come to these conclusions:

- Organisms produce more offspring than needed.
- Characteristics in parents often appear in offspring.
- All organisms compete with others for food, shelter, mates, etc.
- Some organisms are better able to compete than others are.
- The organisms that have the variations that help give them an advantage over other organisms of their species or another species altogether are more likely to survive.
- The best-adapted forms can pass on to their offspring the same advantageous characteristics.
- After a long time, organisms forced to respond to different environmental conditions and competition might develop new characteristics, resulting in a creation of a new species.

In 1859, Charles Darwin wrote *The Origin of Species by Means of Natural Selection*. It is one of those books that everyone knows about but few have actually read. The CBS reality television show *Survivor* is based on the theory of survival of the fittest.

Alfred Russell Wallace developed a theory very similar to Charles Darwin's theory. Although both theories were developed at the same time, they did not know each other. When both men read Thomas Malthus's essay on population, they simultaneously came to the same conclusion. Wallace sent Darwin a copy of his theory. Darwin's reaction was, "I would rather burn my book than that he (Wallace) or any man should think I behaved in paltry spirit." So Charles Darwin sent Wallace's essay on to a publisher. Does not sound like the evil crazy man that creationists portray him as, does it?

The Truth

Listed below are a few of the many facts that make the Biblical story of creation an impossibility:

• Living elephants are descendants of a fairly small tapir-like mammal that lived 45 million years ago. That mammal is called a *Meoritherium,* which was named after Egypt's Lake Moeris, near which its remains were discovered.

• Whales and dolphins have small bones imbedded in the side muscle, which are rudiments of pelvic girdle and sometimes the femur. These bones in some species serve as a point of insertion for muscles but are otherwise vestigial.

• Fossils of Aborigines in Australia date as far back as 38,000 years.

• *Archaeocetes,* the first whale, lived in the Ecocene period, 50,000 years ago.

• An analysis of the alpha chain of the hemoglobin in blood shows identical sequences of amino acids in human blood and chimpanzee blood.

• Humans have vestigial organs, such as tail vertebrae, ear-wiggling muscles, appendix, wisdom teeth and a nictitating membrane (third eyelid).

• The general appearance of more primitive fossil appearing deeper than the more advanced fossil is predicted by evolutionary theory.

• Whale flippers, bat wings, and the human hand all have similar bone structure.

• There are 4,300 species of mammals, 6,300 species or reptiles, and 9,000 species of birds. There are 85 species of *Cetacean* (whales and dolphins). There are ten species of skunk alone. Why would God create ten species of skunk? What is the point? Could it be that different species evolved in different areas?

• Why would God create over 2,000 species of fruit flies and decide to put one-fourth of them in the Hawaiian Islands?

- J.B.S. Haldane pointed out that God must have a special fondness for beetles since there are over 250,000 species of them.
- The first Floridians were Indians called the Calusa Indians about 12,000 years ago.
- American Indians were living at the Clovis site in New Mexico about 9,000 years before Christ.
- There is archeological evidence in Pennsylvania of people dating to about 19,000 years ago.
- There is a diamond mine in Canada dating 57 million years old.
- Recently in Australia a 22,000-year-old statue of a fertility goddess was unearthed.
- A partial skull was found in Chad. It was dated at 7 million years old. It was the size of a chimpanzee but had human characteristics. There will be countless discoveries like this one, helping us answer more questions about the evolution of man.
- Are biologists, naturalists, geneticists, philosophers, archeologists, paleontologists, geologists, geologists, zoologists, anthropologists, museum workers, educators, entomologists, ornithologists, botanists, sociologists, oceanographers, some writers, and many others all working in made up professions?
- Why would God have given us fossils and the intelligence to study them?
- In Lascaux, France, there are famous caves where cave art dates back to 17,000 yeas ago.
- In Chile, homes of people were found and dated back to 13,000 years ago.
- The first domestication of dogs took place with wolves. Man and dog remains were found together in the Beaverhead Mountains of Idaho; these remains were dated to be 12,000 years old. Further proof of this early domestication has been discovered in Europe and Asia.
- Kennewick Man found on the Columbia River in Washington dated to be 9,600 years old.
- All embryos, including human, pass through a stage of development that has gill pouch-like lower vertebrates.

In all the material I researched, I never came across any real facts supporting creationism. Creationists say they have facts to support their theory, but the facts are all twisted and parts are conveniently left out. It is like politics; instead of facts and figures to support one side, the other is just torn down. The evolution side of the creation/evolution debate seemed to have information that was concrete, authentic, and factual. One pro-creation argument was that since there are so many unanswered questions in evolution, it must not be true. Yes, there are many unanswered questions in the evolution story, but new discoveries are being made continually and the pieces of the puzzle are starting to fit together. It is hard to understand how blind faith can simply erase facts and reason. The factual evidence for evolution cannot be denied by reasonable thinking people. What makes more sense having blind faith in story book or studying the facts and using our power of thinking to put them together?

In Charles Darwin's *The Origin of Species by Means of Natural Selection,* in chapter seven, he explains that he could be wrong, that this is just what he thinks. Scientists look at all evidence, even that which could prove them wrong, whereas creationists are only open to information supporting their theory. They flat out ignore proof of evolution.

In the Scopes "Monkey Trial" of 1925, John Scopes, a football coach and science teacher, was accused of teaching the theory of evolution in a school in Tennessee. It was against the law in Tennessee, Florida, Oklahoma, Mississippi, North Carolina, and Kentucky to teach the theory of evolution at that time. He was brought to trial. The judge actually began the trial by reading the first 27 verses of Genesis. Clarence Darrow was the defense attorney and William Jennings Bryan headed the prosecution. Below is a partial excerpt from the trial, just bits and pieces. If you look through the narrow lens of literalism, this is what you sound like:

(Darrow) "You have given considerable study to the Bible, haven't you, Mr. Bryan?"
(Bryan) "Yes, I have, I have studied the Bible for about fifty years..."

(D) "Do you claim that everything in the Bible should be literally interpreted?"

(B) "I believe everything in the Bible should be accepted as it is given there..."

(D) "You believe the story of the flood to be a literal interpretation?"

(B) "Yes, sir."

(D) "When was that flood?"

(B) "I would not attempt to fix the day..."

(D) "But what do you think the Bible itself says? Don't you know how it was arrived at?"

(B) "I never made a calculation."

(D) "What do you think?"

(B) "I do not think about things I don't think about."

(D) "Do you think about things you do think about?"

(B) "Well, sometimes."

(D) "How long ago was the flood, Mr. Bryan?"

(B) "Two thousand three hundred and forty-eight years B.C."

(D) "You believe that all living things that were not contained in the ark were destroyed?"

(B) "I think the fish may have lived."

(D) "Don't you know there are any number of civilizations that are traced back to more than five thousand years?"

(B) "I am not satisfied with any evidence I have seen."

(D) "You believe that every civilization on Earth and every living thing, except possibly the fishes, were wiped out by the flood?"

(B) "At that time."

(D) "You have never had any interest in the age of various races and peoples and civilizations and animals that exist upon the Earth today?"

(B) "I have never felt a great deal of interest in the effort that has been made to dispute the Bible by the speculations of men or the investigations of men."

(D) "You have never in all of your life made any attempt to find out about the other peoples of the Earth—how old their civilizations are, how long they have existed on Earth—have you?"

(B) "No, sir, I have been so well satisfied with the Christian religion that I have spent no time trying to find arguments against it. I have all the information I want to live by and die by."

Mr. Scopes was found guilty of breaking the law by teaching evolution in his classroom and fined $100.00. Science reaches the end of its knowledge and keeps searching; religion reaches the end of its knowledge and just stops. Who wants to be known as someone who does not think about what they do not think about?

If all of the people of the world originated from Adam and Eve, and nothing really evolved, so God made all organisms as is, then they must have been physical messes. According to this theory, all of the current diseases would have been present in those two. Or possibly, if those two were not sick and God just recently created AIDS, cancer, lupus, muscular dystrophy, and all the other diseases, he may have just done it for fun, or to teach valuable lessons to the afflicted or as punishment for sins of the parents or just to broaden people's horizons. Doesn't this sound idiotic?

Not believing in creation has absolutely nothing to do with being a Christian. I believe in God, who started life, and it has evolved into what it is now. Most Christians look at evolution more sensibly than a literal interpretation of the Bible and believe it is symbolic, that God was responsible for creation but it took billions of years, not six thousand. There is no logical reason that God could not have actually started life billions of years ago as opposed to less than ten thousand years ago. It makes no sense at all to believe a literal interpretation of creation like depicted in Genesis when proof indicates otherwise. I cannot believe part of the Bible and not the rest; that does not seem right to only accept part of God's word and not the parts that do not suit me. How can people say they believe the whole Bible to be God's word and every word completely true and then cut their sideburns? Talk about hypocritical! God put the ball in motion and it rolled on from there.

In 1543 Copernicus argued that the Earth and other planets revolved around the sun. His theory countered the current belief that the sun was not the center of the universe. The Catholic Church had a hard time with this; they apparently wanted Earth to be the center of the universe. When Galileo announced that he had proven Copernicus right, he then got into hot water with the Catholic Church. Now everyone believes this theory of the sun being the center of the universe. It is not even a theory, it is a fact. I think evolution is the same as Copernicus's original theory. It will just take a while for some to come to their senses.

The Kansas board of education in 1999 actually eliminated Darwin's theory of evolution from its curriculum. This fact makes me embarrassed to be living in a state next to that state. This was only five years ago! Thankfully, in 2000 the idiotic, backwards decision was reversed. Evolution should be taught in school, especially since there are so many facts to back it up. If a family believes the creation make-believe story, they are free to teach it to their children at home. Maybe these people are afraid that a child may have a thinking mind and question the mumbo jumbo of creation. It is truly amazing that a thinking person can entertain the possibility that evolution did not and is not happening. How absurd!

Bibliography

Tort, Patrick; *Darwin and the Science of Evolution*; Discoveries Book; Harry N. Abrams, Inc.; New York, New York, 2002

MacDonald, Professor David; *The Encyclopedia of Mammals*; Barnes & Noble, Inc.; New York, New York, 2001

Thomas, David Hurst; Miller, Jay; White, Richard; Nabokov, Peter; Deloria, Philip J.; *The Native Americans, an Illustrated History*; World Publications Group, Inc.; North Dighton, MA; 2001

Pugnetti, Gino; *Simon & Schuster's Guide to Dogs*; A Fireside Book published by Simon & Schuster Inc.; New York, New York; 1980

How Carbon-14 Dating Works; http://www.howstuffworks.com/carbon-142.htm

Petrillo, Tom; About Radiocarbon Dating; http://www.geocities.com/CapeCanaveral/Station/8985.rad.htm

Carroll, James; *Constantine's Sword, The Church and the Jews, a History*; A Mariner Book; Houghton Mifflin Company; New York, New York; 2001

http://www.religiousquotes.org/quotes4.htm

Gould, Stephen Jay; *The Book of Life, An Illustrated History of Life on Earth*; W.W. Norton and Company; New York, New York; 2001

Gibbs, Nancy; AOL News; Time Magazine: The Secret of Life; http://www.time.com/time.covers/1101030217/story.html

Berra, Tim M.; *Evolution and the Myth of Creationism*; Stanford University Press; Stanfod, CA; 1990

Horvitz, Leslie Alan; *The Complete Idiot's Guide to Evolution*; Pearson Education Co.; Indianapolis, IN; 2002

Leatherwood, Stephen; Reeves, Randall R.; *The Sierra Club Handbook of Whales & Dolphins;* Sierra Club Books; San Francisco, CA; 1983

Ellis, Richard; *The Book of Whales*; Alfred A. Knopf, Inc.; New York, NY; 1980

Volume Library; Book 1; Section 4; Southwestern; Nashville, TN

Scopes Monkey Trial, http://dimensional.com/-randl/scopes.htm

In the Name of Religion

I believe in God and science, not religion.
-Grissom on the CBS television show *CSI*

Judge not that ye not be judged.
-Jesus

Thou shalt love thy neighbor as thyself.
-Leviticus 19:18, Matthew 22:39

For hatred does not cease by hatred at any time: hatred ceases by love, this is an old rule.
-Dhammapada 15, Buddhism

Peace is the highest value.
-*Tao Te Ching*, Chapter 13, Taoism

All peoples shall love one another and live together in peace.
-Iroquois, *Book of Life*

If you are not part of the future, get out of the way.
-John Mellencamp, *Peaceful World*

The responsibility of tolerance lies with those who have a wider vision.
-George Elliot

The idea that a country or a people could somehow be ordained by heaven to commit unspeakable acts in God's name is insane. Unfortunately, history is full of inhuman acts by religious leaders in the name of their dogma or holy war. Only when the world accepts there are no chosen people or no chosen religions, will we earn the right to call ourselves human beings.
-Zain Winter

Religious belief is a fine guide around which a person might organize his own life, but an awful instrument around which to organize someone else's life.
-Richard D. Mohr, *A More Perfect Union*

Once people get hung up on theology then they've lost sanity forever. More have been killed in the name of Jesus Christ than any other name.
-Gore Vidal

Religion and government will both exist in greater purity, the less they are mixed together.
-James Madison

Religious Intolerance

Throughout history people have used religion to justify injustices, whether it was an individual being run out of a tribe in 20,000 B.C. for being different from other tribe members or on 9/11/2001, when fundamentalist wackos used Islam as an excuse to senselessly murder so many in New York, Pennsylvania and Washington D.C. Two thousand nine hundred and ninety-eight innocent people died on this day. Quotes in the Koran or Bible or any other religious text can be twisted around to serve any purpose.

On 9/11/2001, nineteen men from the Middle East thought they were fighting a religious war and that killing Americans would get them into heaven. First of all, thinking that God or Allah needs your help is delusional or a little "out there." God is God or Allah or whoever else, because he does not need help from mere mortals. To think He needs my help would be slightly egotistical.

2:190 of the Koran says:
The believer is called upon "to fight in the way of God with those that fight with you...but aggress not: God loves not the aggressors."

That passage could be perceived by some as an order to fight for Allah providing that the Americans have already been the aggressors and they were just defending themselves. I don't think so...those people were just plain insane. The Koran also has passages advocating peace and not killing innocent people.

In the Koran, passage 4:29 blows the martyr thing by stating: "Do not kill yourself."

It seems that nobody would be able to use Islam or the Koran to justify killing, but they did. It goes back to people taking a book that supposedly means so much, and just using the parts that are suitable for a specific situation.

The Koran also states in passage 5:48:
"To each (community) among you, we have prescribed a law and an open way. If God had willed, he could have made of you one people. But he wished to test you in that which he gave you. So strive with each other in good deeds."

The same goes for the Bible, which has been used incorrectly many times. The Crusades are just one example of the leaders of the time using the Bible to excuse and defend killing. Killing for Jesus, the man who advocated peace and loving your neighbor, does not make sense. Yet it was done over and over again, more times than this book in your hands reveals. Christianity in history was and continues to be, at a lesser extent, about control.

In human society smaller, less complex societies replaced with more advanced societies. So in most cases, we got smarter as history has moved along...evolution. Certain religions seem more compatible with technology. For instance, Christianity and Judaism are "Westernized." I think that is one of the reasons some Middle Easterners do not like the United States. Islam and Hinduism seem more traditional, not meshing with progress as well.

The present seems more tolerable than the past, but than we get these fundamentalist crazies who want us to go back ten steps like the "moral majority" wanted. Thankfully, it has been listed as extinct since 1987.The Reverend Jerry Falwell was the leader of this political action group that advocated prayer in school, the teaching of creationism in public schools and opposed equal rights, homosexual rights and abortion. If stem cells were in question at that time as they are today, it is certain that they would be opposed to stem cell research. The way things are going the American people might have to deal with this backwoods approach to governing again. Now we have to deal with the likes of Pat Robertson and the Christian Coalition, advocating school prayer. In Matthew 6:1-6, Jesus states that prayer should be private, behind closed doors not public. The Christian Coalition and like groups, now our government, are more concerned with pushing an agenda than actually following the teachings of Jesus. This is more of the...following only certain parts of the Bible that work for me...attitude. The Christian world seems to contain a lot of contradiction and hypocrisy. *If you want your kids to pray in school and they are incapable of doing it themselves, send them to a Christian or Catholic school!* Concerning public school prayer: Who's God will be prayed to? What if you do not want to pray? Can't people pray at home? If a student feels they need to thank God for the school lunch, can't they just do it, without everyone being forced to do it? If a moment of silence is taken at a grade school, what child would not pray for a good lunch or a great game of four square at recess? Kids are kids.

In doing the research for this book, I was shocked at how many times religion was...and still is...the basis for intolerance and cruelty. Most types of religion have been involved, not just Christianity and Islam; although not only being the largest two religions, they seem to be the cruelest. Organized religion, despite all of its favorable qualities, and it has many, has been not about freedom but obedience and conformity.

Countries that have a separation of church and state seem to have less religious conflict. Right now, at this very moment, conflicts about religion are taking place all over the world. Below are listed some of the countries where major conflicts have happened. Communism is listed because communist countries advocate no religion; they do not like people to make decisions for themselves. This list does not by any means reveal all of the places where conflicts have taken place; it just lists a few:

- Bosnia(Roman Catholics, Serbian Orthodox, Muslims)
- China (Communist, Christians, etc.)
- India (Christians, Muslims, Hindu, Sikhs, etc.)
- Indonesia (Christians, Muslims)
- Middle East (Muslims [Sunni, Shiite], Christians, Jews)

- Northern Ireland (Protestants, Roman Catholics)
- Sri Lanka (Hindus, Buddhists)
- Sudan (Christians, Muslims)
- Philippines (Christians, Muslims)
- Tibet (Communists, Buddhists)
- Democratic Republic of the Congo (Christians, non-Christians)
- Angola (Christians, non-Christians)
- Rwanda (Christians, non-Christians)

Religious conflict exists almost everywhere, ranging from Jewish jokes to actual warfare where it is common to kill people. In the year 2000, Pope John Paul II issued a sweeping apology for all the sins committed by the Roman Catholic Church in the past 2000 years. That is a step forward, but just a beginning. It demonstrates the man's character.

Religious intolerance has been around as long as religion has been present. The first two documented cases that I came across were in 399 B.C. and 64 A.D. In 399 B.C., the ancient Greek philosopher Socrates was condemned to death and forced to drink poison for "neglect of the Gods" and "corruption of the young." In 64 A.D., the Roman emperor Nero, in an attempt to persecute Christians, blamed Christians for a great fire in Rome. Many Christians were thrown into pits with wild animals or burned alive. During the 300s A.D., Constantine the Great, an emperor of Rome, thought he received a message from God about a military victory he would gain. He converted to Christianity. During his reign, in 313 A.D., he issued the Edict of Milan, a statement ending persecution of Christians and made the Christian Church legal.

In the year 632 A.D., Mohammed spent the last part of his life trying to convert the rest of Arabia to Islam by using force. These were the first holy wars. Now in the Islam religion there is not just a deep dislike for the West but violence between different sects of Muslims. The Sunnis and the Shiites do not like each other much, so they kill each other? I don't understand how people of the same religion can kill each other because they think slightly differently about some things.

SPIRITUAL CLARITY

Intolerance comes in many forms: the extermination of five thousand Kurds in northern Iraq by the use of a deadly combination of poison gas and nerve agents in the town of Halabjah on March 16, 1988; the severe restriction of dress, freedom and behavior by the former Taliban government in Afghanistan; and the government of Sudan attempting to impose its interpretation of Islam on its entire people. The definition of religious tolerance is to give religious freedom to people of all religions, even though you disagree with their beliefs or practices. Why is this so difficult? It certainly is not a reason for cruelty or killing.

In Northern Ireland, which is 1/3 Catholic and 2/3 Protestant (this is mind boggling, since they both claim to be Christian), 3,500 people have been killed in the past 30 years. 40,000 people have been injured and millions of dollars in property damage has occurred in the Christian vs. Christian fighting. The fighting actually started in the 1600s and has continued. It is still happening. Unbelievable.

China invaded Tibet over fifty years ago, in 1949, and has been attempting to eliminate the Buddhist religion. In a 1959 uprising by the Tibetans against the Chinese occupation, 80,000 Tibetans died. The spiritual leader has been exiled for about 45 years and living in Dharamsala, India. Presently about 120,000 Tibetans are in exile with the Dalai Lama. Monks and nuns have been arrested by Chinese authorities, tortured and held in prison. Just possessing a picture of the Dalai Lama can get you arrested. There are at least 300,000 Chinese troops in Tibet at all times. Over 6,000 monasteries have been destroyed. Monasteries are the places where children attend school and since many have been destroyed, children are forced to attend Chinese schools, which is another attempt of the Chinese to erase Buddhism. The Chinese are trying to put an end to any Buddhists practicing Buddhism. The Chinese language was also made the official language of Tibet. Talk about shoving it down their throats. China likes the profits that it gets from Tibet, which has natural resources of gold, zinc, copper, lithium and other minerals. The Buddhists are in the way of China obtaining these mineral riches.

Then you have your insane fundamentalists of different religions, who feel it is justifiable to kill someone, as long as you have a point to get across. Yitzak Rabin, prime minister of Israel, signed the Oslo Accords in an attempt to end the Arab-Israel conflict. This angered a Jewish fundamentalist, who shot and killed Rabin in 1995. The murdering student Yigal Amir, who was only twenty-five, said, "I shot him because he wanted to give our country to the Arabs." Egyptian President Anwar al-Sadat was assassinated in 1981 by a Muslim fundamentalist for signing the Camp David Accords. Apparently neither one of these fundamentalists wanted peace. In the United States, Dr. David Gunn was assassinated because he performed abortions. His killer was a Christian. Those fundamentalists are all over. Fundamentalists take their beliefs too far; it is the mentality of "my way or the highway." They honestly feel that they are right and the opposing side is horribly mistaken.

The Crusades

The main crusades were a series of military expeditions during the Middle Ages with the main goal being to retrieve the Holy Land (Palestine) from the Muslims. They failed in making the Holy Land Christian but left lots of death, destruction and anger that still remains today.

Karen Armstrong described the crusades in her book, *Holy War: The Crusades and Their Impact on Today's World.* She described how Pope Urban II on November 27, 1095, gave a speech in France calling on Christians to act. People were urged to "take up the cross and kill in the name of the gospel…God wills it." Christian warriors were summoned to recover the holy city of Jerusalem from the Muslims. Several cruel battles carried out in the name of Christianity to advance the power of the Catholic Church. The legacy of violence is still felt today in the conflicts of Christians, Jews and Muslims. The phrase "taking up the cross" was a way of describing fighting in the crusades. The first crusade was referred to as the People's Crusade or the Peasant's Crusade. The first crusaders left northwestern Europe and arrived in Jerusalem in July of 1099. Forty thousand Jews and Muslims were brutally slaughtered. It is kind of ironic to kill in the land of Jesus for Jesus, isn't it? Jerusalem was taken by Christians in the summer of 1099 for a short period of time. One crusader reported the brutal conquest of Jerusalem as killing men, women and children, blood everywhere. He ended with the statement, "It was a just and wonderful judgment of God." *A wonderful judgment of God?*

During the crusades many men, women and children died in a strange effort that really makes no sense, to save religion by killing innocent people. The second crusade was a failure led by King Louis VII of France. A third was led by Richard the Lion-hearted of England, King Phillip II Augustus of France and Emperor Frederick Barbossa of the Holy Roman Empire; it recovered some lost territory but not Jerusalem. At one point on this crusade they slaughtered 3,000 tied up, defenseless Muslims.

In 1198 Pope Innocent III came into power. He prompted a fourth crusade that never actually made it to Jerusalem. But to justify this crusade and others he used a passage in the Bible.

This is Jesus speaking in Luke 19:27:
"But those enemies of mine who did not want me to be king over them—bring them here and kill them in front of me."

The saying "what would Jesus do?" doesn't sound so good at the moment. Jesus seems to say, all who disagree with me should die. That is not very Christian-like. What happened to forgive and love thy neighbors?

In 1217, a fifth crusade took place but it was a failure. The sixth, seventh, and eighth also failed. Jerusalem was lost to the Christians. Many lesser crusades took place. In 1212, a Children's Crusade left France. Thousands died on the way. Many children were captured and sold into slavery. I am still not sure what the point of this Children's Crusade was.

The Albigensians were Christians in southern France who defied the authority of the Catholic Church. They strongly denounced the corruption of the Church and did not uphold the traditional teachings of the Roman Catholic Church. Pope Innocent called for a crusade against the Albigensians in 1208. Twenty thousand Albigensians were massacred in Beziers, France, not just the men but women and children.

More lesser crusades took place: in 1365, the Crusade of Alexandria; in 1396, the Crusade of Nicopolis; and in 1444, The Crusade of Varna. In a very brutal crusade, the Baltic Crusade, non-Christians were crusaded against by the German Teutonic Knights. German bishops began missionary work among the Baltic pagans. The pagans began killing the new converts. In came the knights to eliminate the non-Christians.

A crusade was called against the Hussites in Bohemia in the fifteenth century. The Hussites followed Jan Hus, who was declared a heretic and burned at the stake in 1415. The Hussites revolted against their German Catholic rulers, who were responsible for Hus's murder. Since they revolted against the Catholic Church, a crusade was called against them. This was the mentality then, if anyone caused the Church problems…just kill them…problem solved.

The crusades were organized warfare on behalf of religion and God. They were a prime example of intolerance in the extreme. No Christian converts were gained, no land permanently recovered, only bad feelings spread that are still around today…basically a really big debacle.

The Inquisition

Pope Gregory IX established the Inquisitions courts to arrest, try, and punish heretics. In 1231 the Inquisition began; the Catholic Church continued to do battle with anyone opposed to the doctrine of the Church. The Church controlled everything: thought, art, science, trade, and education. The Church demanded unquestioning obedience. In 1210 and 1215 Papal prohibitions went as far as to restrict the teachings of Aristotle.

Pope Innocent III (what a name!) authorized the use of torture in the Inquisition. Not surprisingly, this increased the confession rate. Accused heretics were encouraged not only to confess but to also reveal other heretics. Anyone could accuse anyone. The Inquisitor would receive reports of others suspected of heresy, sometimes offering rewards in exchange those reports. Those accused were publicly whipped while being led to trial. The Inquisitor would act as judge and jury. The accused had absolutely no rights. Torture was often used to get confessions. People were "relaxed" or ceremoniously burned alive if they were found guilty. Even after the death of the accused, punishment continued; the property of the "guilty" was confiscated, leaving the family in poverty. Pope Innocent III explained this as a way God punished the children for the sins of the parents. Punishing future generations of "sinners" is in the Bible, so it must be fair. Right?

The Inquisitor logic was "better for a hundred innocent people to die than for a heretic to go free." Pope Innocent III declared, "Anyone who attempted to construe a personal view of God which conflicted with church dogma must be burned without pity." With all of this self-righteousness, the accused, who were able, could pay off the Inquisitor to avoid trial and punishment. No corruption there?

The harshest punishment was to be burned alive. The lightest punishment was a sound whipping. Another form of punishment was to be sent on a pilgrimage. Some of these pilgrimages took years. Families of the accused were left behind to starve.

Various methods of torture were used to get confessions: the rack, the hoist, water torture, the pit of snakes, being covered in lard and burned alive, being buried alive, etc. This one seemed the most gruesome to me: first a dish of mice was turned over on the victim's stomach, and then a fire was lit on top of the dish; at this time the panicked mice actually buried into the living victim's stomach to escape the heat. That had to be incredibly painful. The ovens used to kill and torture in Nazi Germany were first introduced by the Christian Inquisition in Eastern Europe. Hitler probably thought of the Inquisitors as creative men with character that he could admire.

In 1326 the Church authorized the Inquisition to investigate witchcraft. By adding witchcraft to the crimes it persecuted a whole new group of people were exposed from which money could be collected. You have to hand it to them; the Church was clever in discovering new avenues to corruption.

Queen Isabella of Castile and King Ferdinand of Aargon, along with Pope Sixtus, began the Spanish Inquisition. The Spanish Inquisition was one of the deadliest in history. It led to the deaths of thousands of Jews, Muslims and more. Many Jews, Protestants and other non-Catholics were driven out of Spain. Tomas de Torquemada became the Inquisitor General or the Grand Inquisitor of Spain. That meant he established the rules of the Inquisition and established Inquisition branches in other cities. He acted as the Grand Inquisitor for 15 years and was personally responsible for about 2,000 deaths.

During the 1500s the Spanish Inquisition turned its fire on the Protestants in an attempt to further unify the nation. The Spanish Inquisition did not end its reign of terror until 1834. One inquisitor in 1578 said, "We must remember that the main purpose of trial and execution is not to save the accused but to achieve the public good and put fear into others."

In 1572, 10,000 Protestants were slaughtered in France. Pope Gregory wrote to Charles IX of France, "We rejoice with you that with the help of God you have relieved the world of these heretics."

In 1613, Galileo advocated the Copernican system of the universe, proposing that the Earth revolves around the sun. Galileo published *Dialogue Concerning the Two Chief Systems of the World—Ptolemaic and Copernican* in 1632. He was ordered by the Inquisition in Rome to stop publication and stand trial. He was later confined to his home until he died in 1642.

The Bible was used to justify all of this. Again, Jesus' own words: "If anyone does not remain in me, he is like a branch that is thrown away and withers; such branches are picked up, thrown into the fire and burned" (John 15:6).

Sounds like justification to burn people alive, doesn't it?

The Inquisition was the most organized effort by a religion to control people. It terrified people into complete obedience. The Inquisition was totally Catholic. Its purpose was to eliminate everyone in Europe who differed from the Roman Catholic beliefs and practices.

Jewish Persecution

Jews have been persecuted since biblical times. Jews are even blamed by some for the death of Jesus. The Jewish elders were not thrilled with his modernistic ideas concerning religion but it was the Romans who killed Jesus. Jesus was Jewish. His followers and his mother, Mary, were Jews. I do not understand the mentality of someone who tells Jewish jokes.

During the first crusade in 1099, there was an unauthorized slaughter of German Jews along the way to Jerusalem. Thousands of Jews were killed in Jerusalem during the crusades.

The Inquisition sought out members of other religions in their search for people to persecute; Jews were fair game. Anyone who had any Jewish ancestors, ate with Jews or had children with Jewish names was a heretic. In Spain in 1492, the Inquisition demanded Jews leave the country or convert to Christianity.

In the thirteenth century, Pope Innocent III required Jews to wear distinctive clothing. Christians frequently rioted against them or refused to sell them food in hopes of starving them. How Christian-like. The Archdeacon of Seville launched a "Holy War" against the Jews. The Black Death Plague took place in 1347-1351. Twenty-five million people in Europe died from the disease caused by fleas on rats. This was about 1/3 the population of Europe at that time. The Church told the people that the Jews were to blame. They, along with the Muslims, lepers and witches, had poisoned the wells, creating disease-contaminated drinking water. Again, the Church found another way to discriminate against the Jews.

Martin Luther, one of the Protestant reformers, was the greatest anti-Semitic of his time. He published many articles on Jews and what he perceived as their lies, In the 16th century he said that Jewish homes and synagogues should be burned. He also said Jews should not be allowed to lend money or travel freely.

Jerusalem is a holy city to all three of these religions: Christianity, Islam, and Judaism. It is special to Christians because Jerusalem holds The Church of Holy Sepulcher. The Church of Holy Sepulcher houses the site of crucifixion, burial, and resurrection of Jesus. Jerusalem is also the site of the Last Supper. To Islam, Jerusalem is the third holiest site, behind Mecca and Medina. The Dome of the Rock is in Jerusalem. The Dome of the Rock is an ancient mosque that has survived over many years; it was built over the spot where Mohammed mysteriously ascended to heaven where he spoke to Jesus and Moses. To Judaism, Jerusalem is the City of David, the ancient capital of Israel. In 1000 B.C., King David conquered the city. He wanted to make it the center of his kingdom and the center of Judaism. David's son Solomon built a temple there.

Jews and Arabs have been fighting over Palestine since long before 1947 when the United Nations established the state of Israel. It became the Jewish homeland but displaced many Palestinians who lived there until 1947. The Palestinians had no place to go and were squeezed into two small areas next to Israel called the Gaza Strip and the West Bank. In 1994 an accord was signed between Israel and Palestine Liberation Organization declaring self-rule in Gaza. But the fighting didn't stop; it continues today. Palestine continually goes into Israel and uses suicide bombing to kill innocent Israelis, trying to take Israel back. As if suicide bombing was a sane way of solving any problem. This is one of the many things bin Laden is angry with the United States about, the U.N. establishing a state of Israel.

The Palestine Liberation Organization was established in 1964. Guerilla leader Yassir Arafat just died so maybe there can be some sort of peace in that area. The PLO regards Israel as an illegitimate state and is determined to establish a Palestine state where Israel now exists. Israel is determined to stay. Both sides need to give a little. But most importantly, the senseless killing needs to stop. Israel is surrounded by Arab states. Jews do deserve their own homeland, but the Palestinians need a home also. Can't they both share? What is the possible reason to oppose an Israeli state and a Palestinian state both existing in harmony?

In the 1920s Jewish immigrants to the United States of America became another one of the groups victimized by the Ku Klux Klan. The KKK is a racist organization of mentally defective individuals who want to keep the United States Christian and white. Still today practitioners of Judaism have to deal with ignorant people acting cruelly, although not as often as in the past.

The Holocaust is probably the most well-known case of religious persecution. It was not a case of persecution but the attempted extermination of entire group of people. The Holocaust showed us what hatred, intolerance, and prejudice can do. The Holocaust is a shocking period in history. It is truly baffling how Hitler came into power and influenced the Germans. He actually thought genocide of anybody not blond and blue-eyed was an attainable goal.

Nazism is a fascist movement organized around the hatred of Jews; Adolph Hitler was the leader of this movement. Hitler began his reign of power in January of 1933. By April of that year he was encouraging the German people to boycott Jewish businesses. The Nuremberg Laws of 1935 increased Jewish persecution. Jews could no longer vote. They were not allowed to teach or work in the government. Jewish students were forced to sit in the back of classrooms. More new rules for the Jews to follow slowly came about. They could no longer go to movies, go to the theatre, go to pools or the beach, go to the zoo, go to museums or ride bikes. They were slowly becoming non-persons. Jews were forced to wear patches on their clothing that would identify them as being Jewish. Soon Jewish children were no longer allowed to attend the schools where non-Jews went. The Nuremberg Laws were used to determine citizenship in the Third Reich (Germany), keep the blood of Germany pure and also to make it known where the Jews stood in the Third Reich. *Kristallnact* (night of broken glass) took place one night when Jewish businesses were attacked.

Jews in Germany fought alongside other Germans in World War I. When Hitler came into power he blamed the Jews for Germany's loss in World War I. He also blamed the Jews for all of the other reasons Germany was not as powerful as it once was. Additional blame was put on the Jews by Hitler for the stock market crashing. Hitler and the Nazi party said, "...the German community derived its strength from the purity of its blood and its roots in the soil. If Germany were to become powerful again, it must root out the unhealthy organisms (Jews, Slavs, Poles, Gypsies and other ethnic groups that were different from pure-blooded Germans) that weaken the nation."

Nazi troops invaded Poland in 1939, starting World War II. In 1940 the euthanasia program for the mentally and physically handicapped began. More ghettos were established. Ghettos were certain areas where Jews were forced to live in cramped and filthy conditions. Many people died due to unsanitary, horrible conditions. In the Warsaw ghetto 500,000 Jews were held. In the Warsaw ghetto an average of 5000-6000 people died per month of starvation, torture, disease, being exposed to cold or being shot. The inhabitants of these awful ghettos were gradually shipped out to something even worse than living in crowded, dirty conditions—concentration camps. There were 27 concentration camps during the holocaust. When initially brought to a camp, the detainees were forced to disrobe, were shaved and then tattooed with an identification number. Families were separated frequently. It was common for people to die of starvation at concentration camps. The Jews were forced to go on death marches and they were medically experimented on, just to name a few of the cruelties that went on.

The "final solution" was put into action in 1942. Death camps were established. If a person was chosen to go to a death camp, the showerheads did not generate water but poison gas. At Auschwitz, a notorious death camp, 12,000 people a day were killed. It was a regular killing factory.

It all ended on May 7, 1945, when World War II was over. All of the camps were liberated and the rest of the world was shocked when the reality of what happened was exposed. The Nuremberg Trials of war criminals began in 1946. Unfortunately, Hitler was not around to face up to what he had done because he cowardly committed suicide. Go figure. Although no punishment could come close to making up for what he had done, he deserved a little torture.

The Nazis and Hitler killed approximately 16 million people during the Holocaust: six million Jews and nine to ten million Slavs, Poles, Ukrainians, Belarussians, gypsies and handicapped. Hitler ranks among the cruelest, if not the master. He caused so much pain and misery in such a short period of time.

Once again, whenever a Jewish joke is told or a slandering comment about Jews is made, the question comes to mind, "Does that person realize that the man they, ever so loosely, base their life on is Jewish?" I know most probably know about Jesus' heritage but what is the deal with the Jewish jokes? Anti-Semitism is discrimination against people of the Jewish faith. Judaism and Christianity are very similar but a central belief in Judaism is that the Messiah is yet to come, bringing peace and unity to mankind. Differing from Jews, Christians believe the Messiah has come and He is Jesus. Where is the peace and unity? What does it matter who believes Jesus is the Messiah or is not the Messiah? A slight variance in religious beliefs does not make one better than the other, just different.

Witch-hunts

Witches are known to eat children and have sex with the devil. Women are much more likely to be a witch than a man, for obvious reasons. Witches are devils agents responsible for all that is wrong. They can be blamed for all misfortune, including famine, illness, a bad crop or even a bad hair day. Find a witch, kill her, and things will start looking up. Any woman who attracted attention for some reason was accused of being a witch, whether the attention was from advanced age, ugliness, a deformity or even extreme beauty. Anyone who practiced healing was a witch because helping a sick person was interfering with God's plan. Healing should come from God, not the efforts of human beings. In witch trials any testimony was believable, even children. Any type of evidence was used no matter how flimsy or circumstantial. Unlimited torture was a reasonable means of getting confessions. Doesn't all of this sound ludicrous? In 1427, Switzerland had the first witch-hunt, and then the major witch-hunting began in Germany, England and France. The Roman Catholic Church created an imaginary evil religion to justify witch-hunts. Pope Innocent VIII issued a papal bull *Summis desiderantes* which promoted the tracking down, torturing and executing of Satan worshipers. During the 16th and 17th centuries over 10,000 accused witches were killed. In Germany alone, between the years 1560-1680, three thousand so-called witches were put to death. Witch persecutions often occurred in areas where Catholics and Protestants were fighting. Catholics found another way to get rid of people who had the gall to believe differently than they did.

The time period from 1550 to 1650 is referred to as "the Burning Times" because there were so many witch trials and executions. In England "swimming a witch" was when the accused, with legs and hands tied, was thrown into water. If she floats she was a witch. If she sinks, she was innocent, but unfortunately dead.

The witch-hunts came to Puritan New England. Laws were actually passed in 1641, 1642, and 1655 against witchcraft. In Salem, Massachusetts, 20 people were executed because they were believed to be witches during a six-month period. In 1692, nineteen people were executed in witch hysteria brought on as a prank by a group of young girls. In Salem, Massachusetts, a man was "pressed to death" by a stone because he refused to address charges of witchcraft in 1690. In the English colonies 40 people were executed for witchcraft between 1650 and 1710.

In England the last witch executed was in 1684. The people of France, Germany, and Switzerland followed, ending this lunacy in their countries. Poland followed bringing an end to the witch-hunts in 1792. The Church did not end witch execution in South America until the 1830s. Since then there have been a few isolated lynchings in Europe and South America. During 1994-1996, several hundred people were accused of witchcraft in the northern province of South Africa and were lynched by frightened mobs.

All of the witch-hunt rational and the actual killing of the accused were, of course, supported by the Bible:

"Do not allow a sorceress to live" (Exodus 22:18).

If it's in the Bible, it must be true, right?

Natives

Hernan Cortés and Francisco Pizarro both headed to the Americas in search of gold. The gold that they did find went back to Spain. It is kind of ironic that the ceilings of many Spanish churches are covered with the gold gained by murder and cruelty. In addition to a hunger for wealth and power, the Spanish were driven by a desire to convert the natives to Christianity. Of course, it was also a perfect opportunity to get some slave labor as a bonus. The Spanish system of colonization was the encomienda system. Landowners were granted a specific type of deed called an encomendar, which entitled them to the labor of the natives living on the land, providing they had converted to Christianity. Mexico did not become independent of Spanish rule until 1821.

Europeans colonized the Canary Islands in 1478. This was beginning of the brutal reduction of natives. This colonization continued to South America, North America, Asia, Africa and everything in between.

The first people in New Zealand were a Polynesian group called the Moari. The Moari were fierce warriors who practiced cannibalism. After the arrival of the Europeans the numbers decreased from 250,000 to 42,000. This decrease was due to disease brought by Europeans and massacre brought on by Europeans also.

Tasmania is a small island south of Australia. The natives to this island were called Tasmoids. The population of Tasmoids was totally eliminated from existence by Europeans, from diseases, to which they had no resistance, and massacre.

Columbus first discovered the islands of the Caribbean in 1492 under the Spanish flag and the Catholic cross. The peaceful Caribs, the natives to the Caribbean islands, almost became extinct being subjected to cruel enslavement and exposure to disease. Columbus himself described how he took pleasure from a native woman after whipping her.

The Arawaks, the natives of the Bahama Islands, welcomed the Spaniards. They were so trusting and innocent, the Spaniards easily accomplished genocide. After a few decades, not one Arawak was left. Not one. Arawaks committed suicide and killed their own babies to avoid whatever Columbus had in store for them. Apparently he had quit a reputation that preceded him if death was a preferred choice than "the great explorer." There were 250,000 Arawaks when Columbus arrived and none by 1650. Why on earth were we taught in school that he was a great man who discovered America?

The Spaniards, led by Hernan Cortés, arrived in central Mexico in 1519 where they found the remarkable city of Tenochtitlán, which was established by the Aztecs in 1325. The Aztecs were the native peoples of central Mexico at that time. Tenochtitlán was located where Mexico City is now. Tenochtitlán was the physical and spiritual heart of the Aztec civilization. Aztec society consisted of three castes to establish social and political organization. They had a centralized government, with a hereditary leader.

The Aztecs had many gods and goddesses of natural forces, the most important being Huitzilopchtli, the god of the sun. Huitzilopchtli was honored by the sacrifice of captured prisoners. Aztecs believed that the world would end violently and they could postpone the ending by feeding the gods human blood and human hearts. The sun god needed food to stay alive. When Aztec warriors conquered other cities to add to their empire, they captured prisoners for ritualistic sacrifice, which was an essential part of the religion. If you were the warrior who captured sacrifice victims, then after the heart and blood were taken, if you were lucky you might get a limb to eat. The skull was used as a decoration in the temple. Men, women, children, and sometimes animals were used in the religious sacrifices. During the time of the Aztec domination 100,000 people were sacrificed.

When the Spaniards, under Hernan Cortés, arrived in 1519, the Aztec civilization was at its height. Spanish and Catholic domination of Middle America began. The Aztecs thought Cortés was the returning descendant of the god Quetzalcoatl. Cortés and his men were wearing armor and were on horseback, so they appeared supreme to the Aztecs. Montezuma, the Aztec king, bowed and handed Cortés presents of gold and precious stones. The Aztecs and Montezuma were defeated anyway. Tenochtitlán fell to Cortés in 1521. By 1525 the entire Aztec empire had been conquered by the Spanish. Now the phrase "Montezuma's revenge" makes sense.

Another group of people thrived in the Guatemala and Yucatan Peninsula area. This group of people originated in 2600 B.C. as the Olmecs. At the time of Spanish conquest they were called the Mayans. It was a highly advanced civilization with art, science and a writing system. There were 14 million people in the Mayan empire at its height. Mayans were pantheistic, meaning they worshipped many gods, and they practiced sacrifice to feed these gods. Mayans would sometimes drown victims in wells. Priests would ceremoniously perform these sacrifices which took place during festivals throughout the year. Those sacrificed were considered fortunate, since they were guaranteed an easy life in the world to come. Sounds familiar.

After the Spanish arrived, 90% of the people died from disease brought by the Spanish. By 1541 the Spanish had subdued the entire Mayan culture. The new arrivals used the encomienda system until 1724, using the natives who had converted to Christianity for labor.

The Inca population lived in South America from 1200-1532. Their civilization was 1,200 miles along the coast in Peru and the Andes Mountains. Incas were deeply religious sun worshippers. Inti, the sun god, was worshipped from the highest point in the village. Pachamama was the earth god, the mother of all. These gods also needed to be fed, but sacrifice was only practiced in times of crisis or for special events. The Incas had a hereditary leader, strict laws, strong centralized government and a strong code regulating all aspects of life. It was a powerful empire, one that had bridges, ferries, irrigation systems, palaces, aqueducts, canals, temples, paved roads, grain storage, towers, stone walls, terraced hillsides, beautiful clothing and pottery. They also mined gold, which led to their demise. Cuzco was the Inca capital, the site of the temple of the sun; the temple was decorated in gold and silver.

At the end of the Spanish arrival Huayna Capac was the Inca leader. Plague swept through the empire killing Huayna Capac. Huayna's son Atahaullpa took over as the Inca ruler. The Spanish fought the Incas that were left after the plague. In 1532, in the Inca city of Cajamarca, Francisco Pizarro captured the Incan ruler Atahaullpa. Pizarro represented the King of Spain. Emperor Atahaullpa was asked to pledge his allegiance to the King of Spain and the Catholic Church. Atahaullpa was told, "We came to conquer this land for the King of Spain and for the Catholic Church. God permits this so you can see the error of your ways and realize that you may become a Christian." When Atapaullpa refused he was taken prisoner. The Spanish asked for ransom and the Incas paid in gold. Pizarro executed Atapaullpa anyway. Apparently, Pizarro was not a Christian man of his word. Then only 180 Spaniards, who had horses and guns, overthrew 40,000 Incas. Horses and guns provide the upper hand. All of the Incas were soon brought under control of the Spanish. Today there are 2-3 million Inca descendants living in the Andes Plateaus.

When the pilgrims first came to America, the Indians had no concept of land ownership. In Virginia in 1607 the Puritans used the Bible to justify acts of cruelty:

"Ask of me, and I will make the nations your inheritance, the ends of the earth your possession" (Psalm 2:8).

SPIRITUAL CLARITY

And to justify the use of force:

"Consequently, he who rebels against the authority is rebelling against what God has instituted and those who do so will bring judgment upon themselves. For rulers hold no terror for those who do right, but for those who do wrong. Do you want to be free from fear of the one in authority? Then do what is right and he will commend you. For he is God's servant to do you good. But if you do wrong, be afraid, for He does not bear the sword for nothing. He is God's servant, an agent of wrath to bring punishment on the wrongdoer" (Romans 13:2-4).

Isn't that Bible convenient?

In North America with the arrival of Europeans also came disease. The initial smallpox epidemic killed 10,000 Cherokees. A tribe of Pequot Indians died in 1637; six-hundred men, women, and children were massacred. There were countless occurrences similar to this one, with natives being eliminated for progress. There was one instance that might be the first act of bio-terrorism; the British gave smallpox hospital blankets to Indians to purposely make them sick and die.

In South Florida the Calusa Indians numbered around 20,000. When Europeans gained control in 1763 the Calusa numbers were down to a few hundred. The Seminole War in 1818 led to the American acquisition of Florida. Eight hundred Creek Indians volunteered to help the United States in exchange for the promise that their families could stay in Alabama; that promise was broken. These are few examples of the horrific acts of cruelty that Europeans committed against the natives of this country that were justified by the Bible. The Royal Proclamation of 1763 began the period of broken treaties. The British agreed to establish a line at the Appalachians, beyond which no settlements would intrude upon the Indians' homeland.

The British so hated and feared the Indians, that on April 10, 1756, the Colonial Council of Pennsylvania began to offer a scalp bounty: $50.00 for an Indian woman's scalp and $130.00 for an

Indian man's, if he was over 10 years old. How could you tell by a scalp only, if the Indian was over 10 years old? How could you tell if the scalps were from men or women? The council must have thought that these fine, upstanding individuals who brought in scalps would never lie.

Andrew Jackson was a slave trader and the most aggressive enemy of the Indians. After he became the seventh president in 1827, 70,000 Indians were forced east of the Mississippi in the Indian Removal. The Cherokee Trail of Tears occurred in 1838; four thousand Indians died on that 800 mile march to their new "territory."

According to Howard Zinn in his eye opening book, *A People's History of the United States*, Native Americans assembled to denounce Columbus in a nationwide protest against honoring a man who raped, enslaved, and murdered natives who greeted his arrival with gifts and friendship. The original European discoverer of North America was Leif Errickson, a Norseman who first landed on American soil, but the landing was not authenticated. It was not Christopher Columbus. America was named after Italian explorer Amerigo Vespucci. Columbus was not looking for America when he first landed here; he thought he was sailing to spice rich Asia. He even cheated a fellow crew member out of an award from Spain, to whoever saw land first. Sounds like a great guy. How can America give recognition to such an unsavory character? Why in school was it taught that he was the great explorer who first came upon America? Why on earth is there a Columbus Day?

Colonists

When early American colonists first came to this land they were attempting to escape religious persecution and then they became guilty of religious persecution themselves. The Puritans insisted that all the colonists conform to their beliefs. Colonists were taxed to support religion and were punished for not conforming. Not attending church was a crime. Many newcomers were banned from settling in this new community.

The laws in New England were so strict, some colonies outlawed certain sports, card playing, plays, eavesdropping, meddling, profane dancing, uncharitableness, tobacco, drinking alcohol, and sex for any reason besides the purpose of making babies within the family. Orthodox Christians believed that sex for any reason other than procreation was a sin. If a husband enjoyed sex too much, he was committing a sin. It was also a sin to enjoy oneself on the Sabbath. So, I guess sex on Sunday was out. In Puritan Plymouth in 1632, adultery was punishable by death. In 1704, Maryland Puritans had a law giving ministers the right to impose divorce on couples perceived as being "unholy."

In the Virginia Colony in 1610, there were religious rules preventing the Lord's name from being spoken in vain. The first offense involved some sort of pain, maybe a severe whipping. The second was a dagger through the tongue. The third was death. The Virginia Colony used the "three strikes you are out" method for keeping colonists at church. The third time caught not attending church was punishable by death. Jamestown in 1618 would jail those who missed service. Massachusetts Puritans would lock church doors to prevent the colonists from leaving early. In 1671, the death penalty was in force for anyone who disagreed with the church. They had mellowed out by 1697 in Massachusetts; atheism was punishable by whipping and then boring the tongue with a hot iron, not death.

On June 1, 1660, Puritan Boston hung Quaker Mary Dyer for entering Boston with strong beliefs about Quakerism. She had been previously banished, but returned. The year before in Boston also two Quakers were hanged for preaching Quakerism. There was not a lot of tolerance at that time. Puritan Massachusetts in 1647 had a law banning the entry of Catholic priests into the colonies. The first offense was banishment and the second offense was death. Where were you supposed to go if banished?

The Puritan colonies participated in the witch hunts. In 1661 Puritan Connecticut hanged 10 people for familiarity with the devil. In 1661, Puritan Maryland actually killed a little old woman and threw her body into the sea to calm a storm. I wonder if that worked.

A New England law prohibited clothing that revealed the ungodly human body. Short sleeves were outlawed for women, preventing the arm nakedness that would inevitably happen. Whoever could take care of themselves the least was the holiest. Not bathing and not combing the hair were supreme examples of holy living. Orthodox Christians thought any care of oneself or healing was not submitting to God's plan, therefore sinful.

On June 5, 1637, Massachusetts Puritans attacked a sleeping Pequot Indian village. As mentioned previously in this book, 600 men, women and children died. The Indians had committed two terrible sins. Living where they should not was the first, even though they lived here first, and not being Christian was the other.

The Constitution was written in 1787 and a Bill of Rights was added in 1789. The Bill of Rights was ratified on December 15, 1791. The first Amendment containing "freedom of religion" was and is a necessity. The founding fathers were brilliant; religion and government do not belong together. I often hear people saying, "Our country was built on Christian principles." Sort of, but now this country is very different than it was. It is a Christian principle to not give women much value, it is a Christian principle to own slaves, it is a Christian principle to plunder and pillage, and it is a Christian principle to punish anyone different from Christians. Do we want to go back to things like they used to be?

In Massachusetts a law in 1653 prohibited Sunday walks to the harbor. They were thought of a being a waste of time. In 1643, garments with ornaments, embroidery, lace, belts, or hats were forbidden. Christians believed that anything that focused attention on the physical body was ungodly. So, on Sunday, if you dressed a little flashy, walked down to the harbor, had sex there, and enjoyed it, you could be burned at the stake and then go straight to hell. Those Puritans were really something; it is amazing that we are taught how wonderful these pilgrims were.

Slave Trade

According to Howard Zinn on page 29 of his fascinating and enlightening book, *A People's History of the United States*, in 1610 a Catholic priest in the Americas wrote to the Church in Europe to ask if the capture, transport and the enslavement of African blacks was legal by church doctrine. The Church replied, "We buy these slaves for our service without scruple." The Bible was used again to support the institution of slavery as part of the divinely ordained hierarchical order:

"You male and female slaves are to come from the nations around you; from them you buy slaves. You may also buy some of the temporary residents living among you and members of their clans born in your country, and they will become your property. You can will them to your children as inherited property and can make them slaves for life" (Leviticus 25:44-45).

Slaves were gained by the conquering of other lands before, during and after biblical times. Ancient tribes and groups of people had slaves all throughout history. As Europeans explored new lands, they captured slaves and stole gold for their churches. Paul instructed slaves to obey their masters in the Bible several times, in Ephesians 6:5, I Timothy 6:1 and Titus 2:9-10...this is the New Testament. Slavery is also mentioned in the Old Testament in Exodus and Genesis as being instituted by God.

Slavery was profoundly immoral. It is hard to believe that the Bible justifies it and says slavery was instituted by God. How can this book be praised and considered God's word if it authorizes such cruelty?

In 1619, the first 20 slaves from Africa arrived in Jamestown. Early on the practice of whipping and branding began. By that same year, around one million Africans had been transported to the Spanish and Portuguese colonies in the Caribbean and South America. So when the Europeans started colonizing North America, they, of course, "needed" slave labor to do the work. An estimated 50 million people were lost to Africa due to the slave trade. At least one million, maybe two million Africans died during transport to America. The Africans were brought to their destinations in cramped and extremely unsanitary conditions. Ten to fifteen million Africans were transported to North America by 1800.

In 1641 the Massachusetts colony legalized slavery. Slavery spread quickly. In 1669, there was a law that said if a slave died from beatings from its master and the slave deserved those beatings for trying to escape or general disobedience, it was not considered murder. From the beginning the Africans were considered subhuman. George Washington himself owned 188 slaves.

President Lincoln was not an abolitionist but did not agree with slavery. His Emancipation Proclamation of 1863 declared the slaves free only in the Confederate States still in rebellion. Ratification of the 13th Amendment to the Constitution in December of 1865 completed the abolition of slavery in the United States.

We are still dealing with the remnants of racism brought on by the practice of slavery. Someday I hope racial equality will sweep the country.

Recent Intolerance

In this section many tragedies are mentioned. These acts were all prompted by religion. Where was that God, the one who controls everything? Did God just get rid of all these people because they were not "good Christians"? The first acts, in this chapter, of cruelty are committed by Communists. Yes, I know Communism is not a religion but it's anti-religion. Communist countries do not promote thinking outside the box. Communist countries only want the people to think like they are told to think. Religions might promote variance in thought about some things.

Joseph Stalin started to train for the priesthood but joined the Bolshevik Party in 1903 instead. Joseph Stalin lived from 1879-1953. He rose from poverty to become the ruler of the largest country in the world. Stalin was the dictator of the Union of Soviet Socialist

Republic (U.S.S.R.) from 1929-1953. Stalin ruled by terror, executing all who opposed him. Twenty million people were executed in the ten year period from 1929-1939.

Mao Tse-tung lived from 1893-1976. In 1949 the People's Republic of China was formed with Mao as the chairman. In the first few years of the Communist's rule, three million people were killed for voicing their opinion. Thirty-five million or more died from starvation due to his method of ruling. Ten million were killed during his rule because they had political opinions varying from Mao.

Kim Jung Il is the North Korean ruler. He was born in 1942 and still remains in power. In 2002, an estimated 200,000 people were in concentration camps; around 5,000 have been killed to date.

In Cambodia, Pol Pot actually spent six years in a Buddhist monastery, two of these years as a monk. In 1975 Pol Pot, as the political and military leader of the Khmer Rouge, overthrew the government, creating the Cambodian Communist Party. During the infamous "killing fields" time period, two million people were killed. In 1998, Pol Pot died in exile in Thailand.

The People's Temple in Guyana was located in South America next to Venezuela. The People's Temple was a socialist utopia. Jim Jones was the leader of this religious community. In 1978, 910 people, including 260 children, drank strawberry flavored punch laced with cyanide and tranquilizers. As his followers died, Jim Jones shot himself, abruptly ending utopia.

In many of Africa's countries for a multitude of different reasons, from tribal warfare to religious conflicts, people are dying in large numbers. Millions of people have died from starvation or illness that could have been prevented if there was not a war or directly from warfare. People have had to relocate to avoid religious persecution in many countries.

In Bosnia, the former Yugoslavia, civil war has killed 25,000 people. The actual civil war was a three-way fight between Catholic Croats, Orthodox Serbs, and Muslim Slavs. The war lasted three years, from 1992-1995. Three million people were made refugees. Twenty thousand have been reported as missing. Thousands of NATO and United States soldiers keep the peace now. Today Bosnia is divided between areas held by Muslim and Croatian armies and the Serbian people.

The Turkish government still denies they had a part in this genocide. In 1915 the Ottoman Turkish authorities directed the slaughter of more than one million Christian Armenians. Muslims in the Middle East do not seem to be very tolerant of members of other religions living in their midst. Since 1979 more than two hundred Baha'I in Iran have been killed. The most recent execution was in 1992. Kurds in Turkey have been killed for being Kurds. Kurds are a non-Arab ethnic group. Twenty thousand Kurds were killed in Turkey form 1984-1991. Iraq has also been Kurd killing.

Then we have the crazy fundamentalists. Fundamentalists can be any religion; they just take things too far. On one interview with Islamic teenagers they were admitting to thinking that they believe terrorist to be brave heroes headed for heaven. Where do they get these ideas? Someone must teach them. In Pakistan, children are taught to hate America. Why is there so much hatred in the Middle East? Hate is not a good thing.

Mohandas Gandhi, a Hindu, led many non-violent protests that helped India achieve its freedom from British colonial rule. Nathuran Vinayak Godse, a Hindu also, stepped forward at Gandhi's daily prayer message; Ganhi gave him the traditional Hindu greeting. The Hindu fanatic pulled a gun and killed Gandhi. It was 1948 and Gandhi was 78 at the time Gandhi was campaigning for tolerance between the Hindus and the Muslims. It appears that Nathuran was not in favor of tolerance.

In Beirut, Lebanon, U.S. Marines on a peacekeeping tour of duty were attacked and killed by an Islamic terrorist. A truck loaded with explosives ran into the soldiers' barracks, killing 241 sleeping marines. A similar attack took place nearby at the French barracks, killing 58 soldiers. Islamic Jihad, a terrorist group, took credit for both attacks.

Abul Abbas, leader of the Palestine Liberation Front, hijacked the Achille Lauro in 1985. The Achille Lauro was a cruise ship traveling from Egypt to Israel. American Leon Klinghoffer was shot in his wheelchair and thrown overboard before the ordeal was over.

SPIRITUAL CLARITY

I saw on the news that Adul died recently...what a shame. A single Israeli, Dr. Baruch Goldstien, opened fire in a mosque killing 29 Arabs and wounding an additional 70 Muslims while they prayed. He was beaten to death on the spot. His mission was to stop peace talks between Palestine and Israel. Why are people from the Middle East so violent? Maybe it is the heat. Heat definitely makes me cranky. Why would anyone think that killing innocent people is going to promote their cause?

Almost everyone in America is familiar with this name now, bin Laden. Osama bin Laden is a wealthy Saudi who financed and ran al Qaeda, which is a terrorist organization. Although it is probably a little more difficult for him to get much done now since he is busy hiding from the United States. Fortunately for him the United States government decided to attack Iraq instead of concentrating on finding him. Bin Laden has declared Jihad or Holy War against the United States. Several of the reasons are, the United States presence in Saudi Arabia, our allegiance with Israel, we are westernized (different from Muslims) and sanctions against Iraq after Desert Storm. Now we can add Afghanistan and Iraq to the list. If these particular situations did not exist, bin Laden would find some other reasons. In 1999 he said to *Newsweek* that "any American who pays taxes to his government...is our target, because he is helping the American war machine against the Muslim nation." *Sounds like a sane man!* It is shocking that anyone would think that after Iraq is stable and we leave...if that ever happens, that terrorism will disappear. We have a democracy in the United States and there are fundamentalists and terrorists here. I'm curious as to how the war in Iraq is supposed to eliminate terrorism. Is the plan to attack all the countries where terrorism exists?

Religious intolerance has always been around causing conflict, from the pre-historic period until today. It is illogical when a Christian, who believes "Love thy neighbor," hates a Jew or a Muslim hates the United States enough to kill when his religion stresses peace. Most of the major conflicts in history have had something to do with religion. More people have died in the name of religion than for any other reason.

Bibliography

Reston Jr., James; *Warriors of God*; Anchor Books, a division of Random House; 2001

Wehr, Jeff; *Religious Persecution in America?*; http://www.hopeint.org/off/9705b.htm

How European Jews Suffered; http://library.thinkquest.org

China in Tibet; http://library.thinkquest.org

Bosnia Civil War 1992-1995; http://www.onwar.com

Modern World History: Stalin; http://www.bbc.co.uk/education/modern/Stalin.htm

Bumbaugh, Rev. David E.; *In the Name of Religion*; www.uc.summit.nj.uua.org

Scully, Gerald W.; *Murder by State*; http://www.ncpa.org/studies/S211.html

Taino; The Story of the Caribs and Arawaks; http://raceandhistory.com/taino/

Robinson, B.A.; *Overview of Worldwide Religious Persecution*; http://www.religioutolerance.org/rt_overv.htm

Flexner, Stuart and Flexner, Doris; *The Pessimists Guide to History*; Quill, an Imprint of HarperCollins Publishers; New York, New York; 2000

Brazier, Chris; *The No-Nonsense Guide to World History*; New Internationalist Publications, Ltd.; Oxford, U.K., 2001

Chal-whan; http://ncafe.com/northkorea/massacure.html;2002

Kim Kwang-in; http://ncafe.com/northkorea/

World Magazine; *Islam and Terrorism, Our Role in the New Cold War*; Nov/Dec 2001

Ehle, John; *Trail of Tears: Rise and Fall of the Cherokee Nation*; Anchor Books; New York, New York; 1988

Ellerbe, Helen; *The Dark Side of Christian History*; Morningstar-Lark: Orlando, Fl; 1995

Maricle, Arthur; *The Inquisition: A Study in Absolute Catholic Power*; http://la.znet.com/~bart/inqui.htm

Religious Freedom: Puritans in a New World; http://www.sonsofliberty.org/sunsociety/puritans.html

Willoughby, Susan; *The Holocaust;* Heinemann Library; Chicago, IL 2001

The Burning Times; http://religiousintolerance. Org/cic_burn2.htm

Diamond, Jared; *Guns, Germs and Steel: The Fates of Human Societies*; W.W. Norton & Co. New York, New York; 1999

Baquedano, Elizabeth; *Aztec, Inca & Maya*; Dorling Kindersley Publishing, Inc. New York, New York; 1993

Zinn, Howard; *A People's History of the United States, 1492-Present*; HarperCollins Publishers; New York, New York; 1999

Armstrong, Karen; *Holy War; the Crusades and their Impact on Today's World*; Anchor Books, a division of Random House; 2001

Nelson, Rebecca; *The Handy History Answer Book*; Visible Ink Press; Canton, MI; 1999

Clarity

I feel that most ministers who claim they've heard God's voice are eating too much pizza before they go to bed at night, and it's really an intestinal disorder, not a revelation.
-Reverend Jerry Falwell

If two men agree on everything, you may be sure that one of them is doing the thinking.
-Lyndon Johnson

Religion is the masterpiece of the art of animal training, for it trains people how to think.
-Arthur Schopenhauer

I don't think we're here for anything; we're just products of evolution. You can say, "Gee, your life must be pretty bleak if you don't think there's a purpose," but I'm anticipating a good lunch.
-James Watson

If you talk to God you are praying; if God talks to you, you have schizophrenia.
-Thomas S. Szasz, M.D.

Conformity is the jailer or freedom and the enemy of growth.
-John F. Kennedy

God is subtle, but he is not malicious.
-Albert Einstein

Teaching a child not to step on a caterpillar is as valuable to the child as the caterpillar.
-Bradley Miller

Heaven and Hell

On *Seinfeld*, Puddy (one of Elaine's boyfriends) was feeling that since he was a good Christian, his entrance to heaven was a sure thing. Elaine, on the other hand, was destined for hell. So Puddy felt it was all right for her to steal a neighbor's newspaper for him to read, since their destinations were already determined. Although he wanted to read the paper, even if it was stolen, since he wouldn't have actually broken the commandment of "Do not steal," he was not sinning. A common aspect of religion seems to be hypocrisy.

Heaven is a bribe and hell is a punishment. Be good and act a certain way and you will be granted admission to heaven and not be condemned to hell. Does it seem fair that entrance into heaven is determined by the location of a baby's birth? If a baby was born into a Christian society he would be rewarded with everlasting bliss, or if he was born into an African tribe than he would head below to burn for eternity. Heaven and hell seem to be based on fear. Fear brings cruelty about. Religion and cruelty go hand in hand.

On *The Bob and Tom Show*, a radio talk show, they did a skit with Harry Caray announcing a baseball game. The setting was the afterlife and the game was played between heaven and hell. Hell's team consisted of Ted Bundy, Jeffrey Dahmer, Hitler, Jack the Ripper, Pol Pot, Stalin, Chairman Mao, Ivan the Terrible and Ghengis Khan. There was a bus pulling up with nineteen Islamic men for Al Qaeda. Harry announced, "Boy, do they look surprised to be on hell's team instead of heaven's team."

The hiding of molestation of children that the Catholic Church took part in is similar to organized crime, obstruction of justice and the covering up of evidence. The underlying problem is the requirement of celibacy. If priests were allowed to marry and have normal homes, there would be no problems or at least fewer problems. The Catholic Church teaches that marriage is a sacrament or holy, yet will not allow priests or nuns to marry. What possible benefit could come from not being allowed to marry besides some goofy symbolism that obviously is not working? Rome states that celibacy is a state superior to marriage. Come on. To Catholics out there, in this metaphor celibacy is a hot object. When a hot object is touched, the brain tells the hand to pull away fast. A change needs to be made. So if several priests cannot handle the celibacy and are acting out by molesting children, a change needs to be made. Maybe celibacy is senseless.

George Carlin's comments on religion put it into perspective. He says that religion actually has people believe that the man in the sky who created everything and now watches over everything has a list of 10 things he does not want us to do. If you break these rules, he will send you to a place where you burn, choke, and scream forever. But, don't forget, he loves you! Believing in hell is simply a mild form of insanity.

Where Was God?

After 9/11/2001, the questions asked by many were, "why did this happen?" and "where was God?" The answer given by some was, "God was helping all those who got out of the towers alive before the collapse, or that he was helping the people who crashed the plane in Pennsylvania, preventing it from hitting a more populated target, or he was helping some of the survivors in the Pentagon make it to safety." How flimsy! Anything can be twisted around to accommodate religion. How does God decide who lives and who dies? The real answer is that God was where he always is, but he does not control everyone's every movement. If some crazed person commits a crime, God certainly does not plan it.

Right after the tsunami disaster I caught the end of a special on CNN, so I cannot give credit because I do not know what it was. The special was about how different religions were explaining the immense wrath of nature. Several answers were about how people were being punished for their sins. How ridiculous! The best answer was from a priest from the Episcopal Church. He said, "It just is something that happens in nature."

Many people believe that God controls all our moves, kind of like a giant version of the game of Life. Below is a minuscule example that God has nothing to do with people's actions or nature:

- In 1835 the Moriori people, who lived on an island east of New Zealand, were killed off by the Maori tribe of New Zealand. The Moriori were hunter/gatherers, not fighters. They solved conflict peaceably instead of fighting. They had very simple technology. The Maori came along with more complex technology and the ability to fight.
- The Australian Aborigines, who are native people of Australia, were driven out of anywhere that newcomers decided would be a good spot to live. Many were killed, many died of disease to which they had no immunities, and some managed to blend into society.
- Eleventh century Mongol leader Ghengis Khan led a journey of conquest and destruction. In a six-month period he killed 1.6 million people.
- Joan of Arc thought God spoke to her and told her to rally the French troops to fight against England in the Hundred Years War. In 1431, when she was just nineteen, she was convicted of witchcraft and heresy. She was burned at the stake.
- The Great Earthquake in China in 1556 killed 830,000 people.
- In 1769-1770 there was a severe drought in India. In an 18 month period millions starved.
- The Yangtze River in China flooded in 1931. Almost four million people died directly from drowning or starvation and disease.
- December 26, 2004, brought a tsunami in the Indian Ocean killing more than 200,000 people in Asia.

These last four are countries where overpopulation is prevalent; was God just doing a little population control? Was he bored and needed some excitement? It is silly to think of God planning everything.

• In America in 1917, whites, angered by the number of incoming black workers, killed 200 blacks. Since the abolition of slavery there have been countless numbers of blacks killed for being black.

• Mount Pele, a volcano in the Caribbean, erupted in 1902. Thirty thousand people were instantly killed.

• In 79 A.D., two cities, one of them was Pompeii, were buried in volcanic ash. Buried along with the cities were all the occupants of those cities.

• On April 20, 1999, in Littleton, Colorado, at Columbine High School, two young gunmen entered the school, shooting to death 13 others and then themselves.

• In Vietnam, in 1975, an orphan rescue mission plane took off. Shortly after taking off a rear door blew open and stuck the tail of the aircraft. One hundred and seventy-two orphans and crew members died.

• A furnace fire in 1908 at a Collingwood, Ohio, elementary school killed 171 children and 10 teachers.

• Timothy McVeigh and Terry Nichols attacked the Alfred R. Murrah Federal Building. On April 19, 1995, a truck loaded with 4,800 pounds of ammonium nitrate fertilizer mixed with fuel exploded outside the building, killing 168 people, including many children in the building's daycare.

• A sleeping pill associated with a birth defect where the baby is born with no arms, its hands coming directly out of the shoulders, was removed from the market.

So when God kills children or makes them deformed and they have not had a chance to sin yet, am I supposed to believe that our righteous God is making them pay for the sins of their parents or grandparents or great-grandparents?

• The wars involving the United States alone: Revolutionary, Civil, Korean, Vietnam, World War I, World War II, Iraq, Afghanistan and Iraq again, prove it is insane to think God controls all. Young men and women are dying just because they are fighting for their country. In the Civil War, 610,000 people died and 471,000 were wounded. That is quite a few people since at that time the United States' population was only 32 million. Why would anyone choose to believe that God does this on purpose?

• In 1986, the space shuttle Challenger exploded, and in 2002 the space shuttle Columbia also exploded. Was this part of the "plan" to prevent people from continuing to learn about the universe? If we are not supposed to question, discover, and learn, why did God give us the brain power to do so?

• Another form of population control that God must of have set up is AIDS. *Does that statement make any sense?* As of 1998, 33 million people have died worldwide of AIDS. I have heard people say that God created AIDS to rid the world of homosexuals. What about all of the others who get AIDS, including babies? My God is not cruel and would not kill people just because they are different. How about yours?

According to Jared Diamond in his book, *Guns, Germs and Steel*, before Hitler came into power in Germany the car he was riding in was hit by a truck. The truck braked in time to avoid an accident that could have killed Hitler. Now if God controlled everything, why was Hitler saved to later attempt the total elimination of the Jews, God's chosen people, according to the Bible?

A high school classmate of mine had two young children. She and her husband went out of town while her mother stayed with the kids. The house burned down killing her mother and her two children. Upon their return, the husband was so distraught that he killed himself. Now, if God plans everything, how cruel can he be? What would be the reason to put my classmate through this? I do not buy that he needed more angels or that he wanted to make my classmate a stronger person by killing her whole family.

I watched the war coverage of the Jessica Lynch rescue. During a clip of her hometown church service, the clergyman said, "God is good." I thought, does anyone actually think that God planned the wrong turn, the ambush of eight of Jessica's fellow soldiers being killed? Or maybe God does not plan desert skirmishes, just rescues. This is some goofy logic. Did the families of the soldiers who died feel that God made a good choice of who lived and who died?

Women

The Episcopal Church was debating over whether or not to have a homosexual bishop in the church and a woman was presenting the side of the argument that did not want to allow homosexuality into the Church. She stated that the Bible declares homosexuality is wrong, which it does. If she really believed everything in the Bible then she would have remained silent regarding church matters. People just pick and choose what they want to believe in the Bible and that is just wrong. You cannot say, "This book is God's word," and then only follow His rules that are convenient. The Bible, New and Old Testaments, do not portray women in a positive way. Women are evil, shameful, weak, and unclean...better seen and not heard. The only thing they are really good for is childbearing. It is astonishing that Christians have the nerve to say any other religion portrays women negatively. Catholics and Jews do not ordain women because they believe God would not want that. Here are a couple verses in the New Testament regarding the Christian Bible's portrayal of women:

"I also want women to dress modestly, with decency and propriety, not with braided hair or gold or pearls or expensive clothes, but with good deeds, appropriate for women who profess to worship God. A woman should learn in quietness and full submission. I do not permit a woman to teach or have authority over a man; she must be silent. For Adam was formed first, then Eve. And Adam was not the one deceived; it was the woman who was deceived and became a sinner. But women will be saved through childbearing—if they continue in faith, love, and holiness with propriety" (I Timothy 2:9-15).

And this is the New Testament?

Also in the New Testament is this passage, which I have heard at a lot of weddings:
"Love is patient, love is kind. It does not envy, it does not boast, it is not proud. It is not rude, it is not self-seeking, it is not easily angered, it keeps no record of wrongs. Love does not delight in evil but rejoices with the truth. It always protects, always trusts, always hopes, always perseveres. Love never fails..." (I Corinthians 13:4-8).

That same book of the Bible says:
"As in all congregations of the saints, women should remain silent in churches. They are not allowed to speak, but must be in submission, as the law says. If they want to inquire about something they should ask their own husbands at home; for it is disgraceful for a woman to speak in church" (I Corinthians 14:34-35).

A couple pages later:
"Wives, submit to your husbands as to the Lord. For the husband is the head of the wife as Christ is the head of the Church...so also wives should submit to their husbands in everything" (Ephesians 5:22-24).

Does not sound like women are in good standing within the Christian church, does it? Leviticus 12:1-8 declares a woman is unclean for seven days after giving birth to a son and unclean for two weeks after giving birth to a daughter. She remains "impure" for 33 days after giving birth to a son and "impure" for 66 days after giving birth to a daughter. Women are blamed for the beginning of sin.

Martin Luther believed the difference in gender, class, race, and belief indicated superior and inferior states of being. In 1533 he wrote, "Girls begin to talk and stand on their own sooner than boys because weeds always grow up more quickly than good crops." He also said, "God formed her body to belong to a man...Let them bear children till they die of it. That is what they are here for..."

Just the idea that women were created as an afterthought from a small piece of God's "special creation" makes it seem that man are superior to women. How can any woman with any self-esteem believe any of this?

It Says That?

The answer frequently heard when questions are asked of religious people, "Humans are finite and cannot possibly understand God," is a cop-out. I think that answer is given when there is no other answer. Faith is the belief in something that is unbelievable, so I guess I am lacking the faith gene. God made a big mistake when he made humans brains so big.

The seven days of creation in Genesis are definitely symbolic, not literal. We have so much evidence against a literal interpretation of the Bible. It is plain to see that the Biblical story is just that, a story.

Adam and Eve were just prototypes for the first humans. They were evolved from ape-like creatures, just like us. If Adam and Eve were the first and only people, having two sons, Cain and Abel, after Abel was killed by Cain, Cain's wife appears. Where did she come from? Cain's rib? Did that section of the Bible get lost? Adam and Eve had another son, Seth. Adam lived to nine hundred and thirty, Seth to nine hundred and twelve, Seth's son Enosh to nine hundred and five, Enosh's son Kenan to nine hundred and ten years, Kenan's son Mahalalel lived to eight hundred and ninety-five years, Mahalalel's son Jared to nine hundred sixty two, Jared's son Enoch only made it to three hundred and ninety five years, Enoch's son Methuselah lived to nine hundred and sixty-nine years and so on down Adam's line. A lot of children could be reproduced since the average life span looks to be about nine hundred years. But that is impossible. Noah did not begin his family until the age of 500. We are expected to take this seriously? Moses died young, at the age of 120 on Mount Nebo. Noah was six hundred when he was given the instructions for the ark. Abraham, Isaac, and Jacob all lived to be over 100. With all the scientific medical advances now, people rarely make it to one hundred. At Biblical times life was so much more difficult than it is today. You were probably fortunate to make it to your thirties. Gray hair was probably not common; most people were probably dead before they reached the gray hair stage.

At 86, Abraham is convinced that his wife Sarah is barren. He fathers a child with Hagar, Sarah's slave. After this Sarah has a child with Abraham. After Sarah dies, Abraham remarries, going on to have six more children. He was like the Energizer bunny. How many fathers past the age of ninety do you know? Abraham is said to be the father of us all: Muslims, Christians, Jews, and everyone else. So we are talking about sibling rivalry gone way too far. I know a few Christians who do not appreciate people of different races; do they honestly believe they are distant cousins to everyone? If we are all related, wouldn't genetics be a mess? That would throw off the fine balance to form a human being. Evolution makes so much more sense.

As quoted before from the New Testament, spoken by the man himself, Jesus:

"But those enemies of mine who did not want me to be king over them—Bring them here and kill them in front of me" (Luke 19:27).

This is a major contradiction. Right before that he says, "Love your enemies, turn the other check, judge not and you shall not be judged." How can Jesus say that he will murder everyone who disagrees with him? Pope Innocent III used this passage to justify his stance on the crusade of 1204. With this biblical quote we could justify killing anyone that gets in our way.

In Romans in the New Testament, Paul, one of the apostles, is speaking:

"Consequently, he who rebels against the authority is rebelling against what God had instituted, and those who do so will bring judgment upon themselves" (Romans 13:2).

Paul seems to be saying that all non-Christians will be going to hell. This type of thinking just generates hatred of other religion. It does not promote religious tolerance. Think like me or you will be punished. *Hmm...*

Lot and his daughters (after the salt incident, which I will address later) sought out shelter in a cave. The daughters wanted children desperately but had no husbands. They were crafty and thought of a way to overcome this problem. They would serve their father wine and then have sex with him. It worked and they both got pregnant. It must have been when incest was not inappropriate. It was later that incest was looked at in a negative way. I wonder if Moab and Ammen, the children or should I say grandchildren, had three eyes. This would be a good headline in the *National Enquirer*.

In a bizarre test of faith, God told Abraham to take his son to Mount Moriah and sacrifice him. An angel grabs his arm at the last minute, saving Abraham's son. First of all, it is just plain psycho that Abraham was prepared to kill his own son for anything, even God's orders. It is also slightly twisted that God would ask this.

God tells Abraham, Isaac, and Jacob that he chooses Israel. So according to the Bible the Israelites are the chosen people. How can religious people who believe the Bible is God's word dislike Jews? Nobody is the chosen people, we are all the same. How can some passages be followed and others ignored, or the New Testament followed but not the Old Testament? Seems hypocritical. The Bible has some ridiculous rules. Here are some:

• Is it reasonable to punish the third and fourth generations of non-believers?
• Divorce is only acceptable if the reason is abandonment or adultery. A divorced person can remarry but is committing adultery if they divorced for any other reason than adultery. What?
• Leviticus forbids the planting of two types of seeds in one field.
• Leviticus forbids wearing a garment of different materials.
• Leviticus tells us what we can eat and what we cannot eat. All "unclean" animals are rabbits, pigs and shellfish. No oysters, crab, shrimp, lobster, scallops or clams. This is just plain wrong! Seafood is important.

- Leviticus also says men cannot cut their sideburns.
- Leviticus forbids a man to have sex with his wife while she is menstruating.
- If a man curses his parents he must be put to death.
- If a man has sex with animal, the man and animal must die.

Blah, blah, blah…

Leviticus 18:22 says, "you shalt not lie with a male as a female, it is an abomination." And in Leviticus 20:13, "if this is done, the punishment is death."

What happened to love your neighbor? Or is that only true if your neighbor is just like you?

Violence in the Bible

After God tried to get the Egyptian Pharaoh to release the Israelites by using a drought, a plague, bloody water, infestation of frogs, locusts, flies, gnats, death of livestock, boils, hail, and three days of darkness, he resorted to baby killing. God was serious and the Pharaoh was stubborn. You do what you have to do. His plan was to kill the firstborn in all homes in Egypt with the exception of the Israelite homes because the front doors of these homes would be marked with lamb's blood. There is a Jewish holiday known as "Passover" to celebrate the time that God freed the slaves by killing the Egyptian firstborn sons and passing over the Jewish homes. My question is, since God is all-knowing, why would He need the Jewish doors marked? Wouldn't he just know who was who? The Pharaoh's son was killed; he finally relented and let the Israelites go.

The sea was parted so the newly freed Jews could pass through. Moses was told to wave his hand and then the sea filled back over the Egyptian soldiers, drowning them and the poor horses. These men were just doing as their leader told them to do, just following orders and God killed them for it. This sounds just like bin Laden saying that all Americans should die for the government's perceived wrongs.

Lot's wife was murdered by God for turning her head and looking the wrong way. She looked back at the cities of Sodom and Gomorrah even though God said not to, and she was turned to a pillar of salt. I understand she disobeyed, but isn't this a tad bit harsh? What about all those babies and children in the two cities? Were they just paying for the sins of their parents?

The Born Again Skeptics Guide to the Bible by Ruth Hermence Green lists 70 mass killings ordered by God or carried out by God. Psalm137, lines 8 and 9, God is asked to praise those who bashed Babylonian infants into the rocks. Those horrible Babylonian infants must have really deserved it. Anyone who supports the not using of birth control but understands the killing of babies because it is in the Bible needs to really examine themselves because they are nuts. Actually, birth control does nothing close to killing babies, but that is what those wacky fundamentalists think. Israelites invaded Canaan and with God's instruction exterminated seven nations in widespread acts of mass murder:

"At that time we took all his towns and completely destroyed them—men, women and children. We left no survivors" (Deuteronomy 2:34).

That was the defeat of Sihon King of Heshbon.

Next, on to Og King of Bashan:

"We completely destroyed them, as we had done Sihon King of Hesbon, destroying every city—men, women and children. But all the livestock and the plunder from their cities we carried off for ourselves" (Deuteronomy 3:6-7).

The Tale of an Ark

The ark must have been much larger than the dimensions in the Bible, because 450' x 75' x 45' simply would not have worked. There are 350,000 kinds of beetle alone. Not counting all the other kinds of insects, that is a lot of cages. The cages had to be made very well considering at that time there were not items for cage construction like today, no glass, plastic or metal. That must have been some hard work just dealing with the insects. Each bug has a different diet and lives in a different environment.

There are 925 species of bats, 200 species of primates, 192 species of hoofed animals, and 270 species of carnivore, just to name a few. Now wouldn't it have been difficult to keep the carnivores from thinking that all the other passengers, including Noah and family, were brought along as their food? An all you can eat buffet.

There are 2,000 different types of rodents. Everyone who has ever had a rodent for a pet knows that you cannot keep them in a wooden cage, they chew through wood, so what did Noah do? It would take a really well-built wooden cage to keep a lion inside from eating the antelope next to it. Or was this when we are supposed to believe that the big cats and other carnivores ate grain and nothing was caged? Have you seen the difference between a cat's teeth and a cow's teeth? Do you know why zoo animals are kept in cages? Not all animals get along. How did Noah get polar bears and kangaroos to Palestine?

Enough food for all of these creatures is hard to imagine. Fresh meat for the carnivores would have been difficult especially since there was no refrigeration at time. Certain types of plant food, kept fresh for different animals, including lots of fresh fruit, would need refrigeration. Although anything refrigerated for 150 days would be rotten anyway. Lettuce wilts and turns brown after a week. Meat gets putrid in a short time. Where did Noah get eucalyptus leaves for the koala bears? Eucalyptus leaves are the only food koala bears eat. Maybe Noah used tough love and made them eat hay. There would be plenty of water but collecting enough rainwater and delivering it daily to that many creatures would have kept the whole family busy. They would not have time for anything else, like feeding the animals or cleaning cages.

What about the dinosaurs? There were 668 species of them. Some say that the fossils we find today are the dinosaurs that died in the flood. Why weren't they allowed onboard? Did God just decide that He did not want them around anymore? Why doesn't the Bible mention them? Could it be because they were long extinct by then?? I have also read that they were onboard. How ridiculous! Has anyone seen Jurassic Park? Apparently not the people who think they were onboard. The idea that the large animals were taken onboard as eggs or infants is crazy also. How could they get all that specialized milk and store it without refrigeration? Who would keep all of the eggs incubated? How would they incubate eggs without electricity? The idea of saltwater and freshwater mixing also brings questions about. It cannot be done with the expectation that either saltwater or freshwater fish will live. Fish are sensitive. The bacteria levels in the waters would be so high with all the floating dead animals, birds and people. Fish are extremely picky about their environment. The excrement onboard must have just been dumped over the side, unless they had millions of dung beetles. Wait a minute, that could not be because the Bible says there were only two or seven of each species (depending on whether dung beetles are considered clean or unclean; I vote for unclean) onboard. What about all the cetaceans? They would have all died also with that nasty water. So where did all the fish and marine mammals that are around today come from?

This was an incredibly disgusting way of ridding the world of all the sin and it obviously did not work. Why did all of the animals except one pair have to die? The babies who died were being punished for their parents' sins, right? Then after all this, what was the point of having Noah sacrifice some of the birds and animals in Genesis 8:20?

Stem Cells

This chapter is included because it is an example of religion interfering in the good of mankind. President Bush made a decision based on his religious feelings. An Evangelical Christian has no business making decisions based on religion for the whole country when not everyone feels like he does. What were people thinking? I can understand where he is coming from not, wanting to create life for research, but not using what is already there is ridiculous.

Half of all Americans could benefit in some way from stem cell research:
- One million children with juvenile diabetes.
- Eight million people with cancer.
- Fifty-eight million people with heart disease
- Four million people suffering from Alzheimer's disease.
- Ten million with osteoporosis.
- Two hundred and fifty thousand people paralyzed with spinal cord injuries.
- Thirty thousand victims of Lou Gehrig's disease (ALS).

People with severe burns, hereditary spastic paraplegia , Parkinson's disease, muscular dystrophy, multiple sclerosis, digestive tract diseases, birth defects, stroke victims, primary lateral sclerosis and a multitude of other physical problems could be helped with stem cell research.

"Could" is the operative word in the last paragraph. We do not know stem cells potential yet. But don't we owe it to the already living humans to find out?

One-third of all fertilized eggs spontaneously abort and are expelled from a woman's body. We do not have funerals or mourn these embryos. Could it be that they are not really "babies" yet? Only when it is convenient do people call these clumps of cells babies or fetuses. They are not fetuses. Stem cells are retrieved when the embryo is about five days old. There is a big difference between an embryo and a fetus. The thought of not using a five-day-old clump of cells that is going to be thrown away is irrational. It is not a person. It is life but so is a cow headed for the slaughterhouse or a stalk of corn.

The biological clump of cells used in embryonic stem cell research is smaller than the period at the end of this sentence. It has no nervous system and is not able to experience any senses or feelings. That means no soul. It has no plans to become a human. What it does have is the potential to cure diseases for millions of people. It is just a possible cure, but we need to find out, and to do that we need to do more research.

In fertility clinics around the country, extra embryos are sitting in freezers awaiting disposal, if not kept for the possible creation of a sibling. The extras are thrown away with the informed consent of the parents. Many couples opt for disposal instead of having that embryo used to create a child for someone else because they do not want someone else raising their child. Multiple embryos are created to insure they get at least one that is viable. Shouldn't these be used to help others instead of being thrown away? What is the possible benefit of throwing them away instead of using them for research? Does a five-day-old clump of cells have the same moral value as a child?

Stem cells are cells that can replicate themselves and also generate more specialized cells as they multiply. Stem cells occur at all stages of human development from embryo to adult, but their versatility and abundance gradually decrease with age. Embryonic stem cells may be able to become any of the 200 different types of specialized cells that make up the body. An embryonic stem cell could become a cardiac muscle cell, nerve tissue, connective tissue, bone marrow, bone tissue, a skin cell, blood components, liver tissue, part of the digestive tract, skeletal muscles, etc. Adult stem cells appear to be less versatile but more versatile than we originally thought. They possibly could be used for organ transplants. We need more research on all types of stem cells.

Most of the body's specialized cells cannot be replaced naturally if damaged or diseased. Although some of the conditions or injuries can be treated through transplantation of entire healthy organs, there is a shortage of donors. Remember Walter Payton? This has always been puzzling to me, the idea that someone would not want to donate their organs after death. They don't need them anymore and just by donating a life could be saved. The alternative is to have the organs rot.

To sum up the question of using embryonic stem cells for research instead of throwing them away: To put it bluntly, why would anyone rather a few cells be tossed in a bio-bag as opposed to helping another human live to his or her potential?

My Clarity

My initial goal in doing this research and putting this information together was to better understand spirituality and religion because, to be honest, they were always difficult subjects for me and I really had no clue. I wanted to know what it all meant. I never understood unconditional faith and what benefits people got from attending church regularly. The big question for me was…Do people need to go to church every week to be "good people"? I always felt that I was missing a vital part of myself. I was missing out on something. Now I understand that I am just not a good "follow the leader" player and that is just fine. The goal to answer the big question for me was answered and now I want to share this knowledge with my son and others.

Once you bring a child into this world you have an immense responsibility. That obligation extends far beyond providing food, shelter, and clothing. As a parent, I have a duty to help Matthew travel on his journey to adulthood armed with as much knowledge about certain aspects of life as I can, two of those aspects being religion and spirituality. He may believe, and probably will, that Christianity is for him but to make that choice, it is only fair to make him aware of other ways of thinking. Now this information may be presented in a slightly biased manner, after all, Matthew's parents are only human. I would really feel as if he was not given the whole picture, if I just told him what to believe. He is not just like me or his father, he is his own person. It is not wrong to only teach your children your own religion if that is what you truly believe, but it is wrong to tell them that is the only correct way to believe. With my questioning nature, I feel I owe it to Matthew to expand his horizons. I am not so closed-minded to the possibility that another group of Christians or another group entirely might fit into his lifestyle more so than the Episcopalians. I say Episcopalians because that is the church that my husband Mark, myself and my son, Matt, have all been baptized in. I can share with him what I believe and his father can share what he believes, but Matthew has a mind of his own; when he is older he can make whatever decision suits him.

I also feel that it is important to learn about various religions' histories and the way that different religions interact with each other. This clarity has the potential to make my son's travels through life smoother and more peaceful. I would prefer, if Matthew inherited my questioning mind, and I think he did, that he does not struggle with the whole spirituality/religion issue like I struggled.

In regard to helping others achieve clarity, I assume that I am not the only one dissatisfied with the knowledge that I had about spirituality and religion, which was not much. Almost all of the many people I talked to just believed what they were told to believe, so I think that it would benefit many to do some reading and learn what is out there. Who wants to be categorized along with the man who said, "I do not think about what I do not think about?" It is a perfect choice to choose what you have already been exposed to. It is also a perfect choice to think differently about some things. There is a lot out there. Maybe we, as a whole, can be open to new things and come to the realization that things might not be as they seem. Tolerance, acceptance, and questioning are good things. Life is wonderful and we need to experience it all, not just our own little corner of the world.

Does it really make sense that the creator of the whole universe would be the same God in our own religion and not any other, so everyone else is wrong? Organized religion seems to be similar to lemmings in the Arctic heading to a cliff and falling into the sea just because the lemming in front of them and their ancestors did the same thing. Religion has been and is an excuse to hate and kill. Religion is also a way for humans to relate to God and a behavioral guide for those who need it. It is and always will be hard to understand why some people need rules to tell them how to behave in simple matters, like being kind to others. I do not understand how anyone would need church to tell them how to act in a caring manner but some obviously do. Religion can outline a path toward a specific goal. It can answer the mysteries of existence. It can tell us how to achieve a meaningful life. It creates comfort for the faithful. Religion is definitely the most powerful force in history. Unfortunately, religion has been and is a way to justify bigotry, racism and sexism. Ignorance, lack of contact, and the belief that your religion is the only right one and everyone else is highly mistaken can lead to fundamentalism and that can be dangerous. It is important to have harmony among different religious traditions. As human institutions, all religions are capable of corruption.

As a child, I was not brought up with any religious background but I was taught to appreciate the world and people around me. Maybe things would have been easier for me if I had been brought up with a religious background. I would have gone through a lot less confusion. But to be honest, I feel things turned out wonderfully for myself; it just took a while to figure things out. The natural world always seemed so much more believable than going to church every Sunday or reading the Bible. I just could not bring myself to worship a man who had been tortured and nailed to a cross wearing a crown of thorns; it always seemed a little morbid. Life is much too beautiful to worship death. I was just not expected to accept things because my parents accepted them. Real life and evolution made so much more sense. I am a fact and science believer, that is just who I am.

There is a natural tendency to associate spirituality with religion, but they are very different. That, I did not know. Religion is an organized system of beliefs in and the worship of God or gods. Spirituality is finding your own authentic self. Each individual needs to find their own way to spirituality and to religion, if they choose. Some people will be perfectly content to just believe what they are told to believe and some will need more. Either path is fine. There are so many problems in the world today. Religion should help reduce conflict and suffering, not be another source of conflict. God definitely cannot plan everything because of all the horribly cruel events that studying history reveals. Unless God is cruel, and I do not believe that is the case. I do not picture him standing in the heavens holding a spiral notebook and a sharpie saying, "Now it is time for number 68257ZIAS to have a heart attack and die while working out at the gym; #222375KKDR should kill numbers 735096SPFR and 988378ADPA and 257394ZWQL, maybe a drive-by shooting, yes, that would be good; now #339119DLHW will discover a lump and be diagnosed with breast cancer; she will ultimately die because her family needs a growing and learning experience, etc…" I don't think so.

His holiness, the Dalai Lama, talked about in one of his books, *The Art of Happiness*, the fact that religious beliefs are good but even without a religious belief, people get by. In some cases they can even manage better. Beliefs or no beliefs are each person's right. He added that there is another level of spirituality that is what he calls basic spirituality—the basic human qualities of goodness, kindness, compassion and caring. This kind of spirituality is essential. He considers this second level of spirituality to be more important than the first. I believe that also. Society would be a mess; no one would be happy without the presence of these basic spiritual values. A church is not necessary to achieve these values.

It seems important for people to identify themselves as a Christian or to describe someone else as a Christian. It is a pet peeve of mine when someone is describing another person and says, "He's a good Christian." What does that mean? That really does not do much to explain about someone's good qualities. Being a "good Christian" means nothing. I would much rather hear how they helped another human being or an animal…that would do a lot more for describing their character. Being a Christian or absorbed in some other religion tells me nothing about what kind of person someone is. After all, Joseph Stalin was heading for the priesthood. Pol Pot was a monk.

I know plenty of shabby people who are Christians and plenty of good Christians also. The same goes for several religions. The point being that religion does not always produce good people, although it can be a path to goodness. There is a lot more than just participating in a religion to be decent.

George W. Bush wants to mix religion in with government. Isn't that what we are fighting against in the Middle East, religion and government being so intertwined? I have so much more to say about this but I will not.

The Bible and all religious texts do have one main parallelism and that is "The Golden Rule." If everyone lived by this one simple phrase, just think how much kinder and gentler the world would be. Almost every religion has this message in some form: Baha'i, Hinduism, Judaism, Christianity, Buddhism, Zoroastrian, Islam, Wicca, Jainism, African religions and more. Treating others as you want to be treated. Just that one sentence, if followed by everyone, would change the world. And not just followed one day of the week but all seven.

There is a God and he created life. It had to come from somewhere. Our higher power or God creating it just seems to make sense. Spontaneous generation is a little hard to believe. Then that newly started life evolved to what it is now. The Bible is just an epic novel about the rise and fall of the people of Israel and their continuing relationship with God. I do not believe it is the word of God. *I can hear you gasping.* Being a good person has absolutely nothing to do with going to church. You are no better than anyone else and no one is better than you, at least as far as beliefs, nationality, sexuality or skin color goes. Live and let live!

I have a personal relationship with God but I do not need a storybook to tell me how to do it. I prefer to think of God as all-loving instead of all-knowing. I pray to God. I pray for others frequently, but never for myself. It seems selfish to pray for myself.

A Christian has been defined as a person who has accepted Jesus as their savior by some and then defined more loosely by others. I feel that Jesus was a great man but most things in the Bible seem to be false, so I have to admit to questioning this also. It just does not seem right to believe the Jesus story but nothing else in the Bible. So if some feel I am a non-Christian so be it, but I do not believe it does. *Do I hear more gasping?* I still refer to myself as Christian and I am not sure why. Why does there need to be a rule, stating who is Christian and who is not? Who is the maker and enforcer of this rule? Not God, he loves all people and is not concerned with rules. Can I declare myself as an independent as far as religion goes? Like if I want to vote for the best candidate for a political office not just the person my party selected. My voter registration card declares me as an independent. Maybe we need cards stating our religion. A religious independent sounds good to me. It is a strong belief within myself that the main focus should be the good within each individual. We should all be responsible for what kind of people we are.

I simply cannot associate myself, in good conscience, with organized religions that have behaved so badly in the past and still do not treat everyone equally and properly. I cannot place a book up on a pedestal that advocates cruelties and contradicts the truth.

I recently read an biography about Jerry Seinfeld where he talked about his feelings concerning religion. He said he was very interested in Eastern thought and likes to explore a lot of different ways of thinking. To him, life is like flipping around the TV set...It's there for him, but he does not embrace things completely. He dissects them and takes what he wants.

Millions worldwide suffer from malnutrition and the threat of starvation. One-third of the grain in the world is used to feed animals being fattened up for slaughter. The amount of grain fed to animals being raised for slaughter is higher in the United States than other parts of the world. A vegetarian diet reduces the risk of heart disease and cancer. It also makes weight loss easier and lowers cholesterol. Animals are given hormones and antibiotics, both of which humans can do without in excessive amounts. An added benefit to being a vegetarian is that we do not have to worry about mad cow disease. Vegetarianism shows a respect for all of creation or life. The following quotes are from the Bible; if you believe it is God's word, then it appears that he did not have some of the cruel practices of factory farming in mind:

"A righteous man has a regard for the life of his beast" (Proverbs 12:10).

"The Lord is good to all, and his compassion is over all he has made" (Psalm 145:9).

SPIRITUAL CLARITY

The reason I brought this up has nothing whatsoever with trying to convert anyone to becoming a vegetarian. I honestly do not care whether other people eat meat or not. I personally just choose to not have an animal killed for the sole purpose of me eating it. I cook meat every night for my husband and son; that is their choice to eat it, not mine. It does not bother me at all to cook meat for them or the fact that they chose to eat meat. I am just trying to point out another way in which the Bible followers are being hypocrites, by following only certain parts of the Bible that are convenient. For someone who really enjoys a good steak, it would be inconvenient to not eat meat. Isaac Bashevis Singer said," We are all God's creatures...we pray to God for mercy and justice while we continue to eat the flesh of animals that are slaughtered on our account is not consistent." Jesus spread a message of compassion, love and mercy. He said, "Blessed are the merciful."

Another problem I have with a lot of religions is self-righteous people saying that homosexuality is wrong, according to the Bible. The same part of the Bible that states homosexuality is wrong, states not to wear a garment made of two different materials. How can an individual believe only one of two statements next to each other? Could it be that no one actually believes the Bible is God's word, they are just too afraid to admit it? Could it not be God, but just self-righteous people who have a problem with homosexuality? That sounds like the answer.

My hope is that everyone would achieve spiritual clarity and then I think we could finally have a peaceful world, maybe in another couple hundred years. It seems like most conflicts between countries and within them have some tie to religion. To achieve clarity we need a more extensive view of religions.

We also need to just not passively hope for a peaceful world but to actually do something. Each little step in the right direction helps. These small steps may be donating blood; becoming an organ donor; being a bone marrow donor; volunteering at an animal shelter like Best Friends in Utah, which is a large no kill shelter; buying a goat or some other animal from Heifer International, which takes the purchase and gives it to a needy family in the world; volunteering anywhere that needs it; giving a child a home who desperately needs a home; adopting a pet; or sending money or goods to those who need it. Whatever makes you feel as if you are doing a positive thing for someone or something other than yourself. Sending money to a church so that people as well off as yourself have a place to go to worship is not the same thing as giving the money to someone who needs food or clothing. It is like spending 43 million of privately donated money for an inaugural celebration while the troops who are at war right now are underpaid and under-armored. Boy, that needed to be toned down a tad. Kindness counts. Churches do a lot of beneficial things for charity, but sometimes that seems to be a small part of church when helping others should be the main focus. Just think what would happen if you took all of that money you have sent in the mail to your church once a month or the money you dropped in the collection plate and used it to really help. We could probably end starvation that way. Or get medication and medical help for those with AIDS in Africa. We could do a lot.

Why do people who believe a certain way find it necessary to make others think like they do? Another problem with religion: people should just believe what they are comfortable with and leave everyone else alone. Religion is a very personal thing. Spirituality is also very personal. I have a friend who is constantly telling me that my beliefs are wrong and he is praying for me to see the light. That hopefully someday I can become a true and proper Christian. It's getting old; give me a break! He means well but I feel totally comfortable with my thoughts and my beliefs.

I saw on an Internet website recently, Laura Lind, the author, described herself as Orthodox Seinfeldism; sign me up for that one.

Bibliography

His Holiness The Dalai Lama and Howard C. Cutler, M.D.; *The Art of Happiness*; Riverhead Books, New York, New York; 1998

Russell, Bertrand; *Religion and Science*; Oxford University Press; 1997

Yancey, Phillip; *Reaching for the Invisible God*; Zondervan; Grand Rapids, MI 2000

Kreeft, Peter and Tacelli, Ronald K.; *Handbook of Christian Apologetics*; InterVarsity Press, Downers Grove, IL; 1970

Time Magazine; *The Legacy of Abraham*; David Van Biema; September 30, 2002

Finkelstein, Israel and Silberman, Neil Asher; *The Bible Unearthed*; The Free Press: A Division of Simon & Schuster; New York, New York; 2001

His Holiness the Dalai Lama; *Live in a Better Way*; Penguin Congress; New York, New York; 1999

Evans, C. Stephen; *Why I Believe*; InterVarsity Press; William B, Eerdams Publishing Co.

Russell, Bertrand; *Why I Am Not a Christian*; Touchstone Books, Simon & Schuster, 1957

McLennon, Rev. Scotty; *Finding Your Religion*; HarperCollins; New York, New York; 1999

Berg, Marcus J.; *Reading the Bible Again for the First Time*; HarperCollins Publisher, Inc.; San Francisco, CA; 2001

Reeve, Christopher; *Nothing is Impossible*; Cambria Productions; Random House; New York, New York; 2002

Stem Cell Research Foundation: What's New; http://www.stemcellresearchfoundation.org

Stem Cell: A Primer; http://www.nih.gov/news/stemcell/primer.htm

Redfield, James; Murphy, Michael and Timbers, Sylvia: *God and the Evolving Universe*: Penguin Putnam, Inc.: New York, New York: 2002

Smolker, Rachel; *To Touch a Wild Dolphin*; Anchor Books, a Division of Random House; New York, New York; 2002

Flexner, Stuart and Flexner, Doris; *The Pessimist's Guide to World History*; Quill, an imprint of HarperCollins Publishers; New York, New York, 1992

Diamond, Jared; *Guns, Germs and Steel*; W.W. Norton and Co.; New York, New York; 1999

Zinn, Howard; *A People's History of the United States: 1492-Present*; HarperCollins Publishers; New York, New York; 1999

Oppenheimer, Jerry; *Seinfeld: The Making of An Icon*; HarperCollins Publishers; New York, New York; 2002

Kimball, Charles; *When Religion Becomes Evil*; HarperSanFrancisco; San Francisco, CA 2002

Printed in the United States
35719LVS00002B/15